4/29/13

Dear Ingrid,

Even though we haven't met, you are a friend of Nancy's, and thus a friend of mine. I hope that these words will be a warm hug for you. Please know that all nine of us in these pages understand this difficult journey. We have all felt the pain — and have been amazed at our resilience & resourcefulness, as we go through each day. And so will you!

With best wishes — & I hope we meet someday —

COMMON THREADS
Nine Widows' Journeys Through Love, Loss and Healing

by
Diane S. Kaimann

Baywood Publishing Company, Inc.
AMITYVILLE, NEW YORK

Library of Congress Catalog Number: 2001043502
ISBN: 0-89503-264-3 (cloth)

Library of Congress Cataloging-in-Publication Data

Kaimann, Diane S., 1939-
    Common threads : nine widows' journeys through love, loss, and healing / by Diane S. Kaimann.
      p. cm.
    Includes bibliographical references (p.).
    ISBN 0-89503-264-3 (cloth)
     1. Grief. 2. Bereavement- -Psychological aspects. 3. Loss (Psychology) 4.
Husbands- -Death- -Psychological aspects. I. Title.

BF575.G7 K35 2001
155.9'37'082- -dc21   2001043502

Table of Contents

DEDICATION

To nine good men . . .

You left us too soon.
We had not enough time,
Not enough hours, not enough days, not enough years.
Instead you left us gifts:
Memories of love, laughter, struggle,
Spirit, strength, victory,
To help us live without you.
You taught us lessons we only now are coming to appreciate.
You are gone.
But you are with us,
Yesterday, today, tomorrow.

Foreword

My husband Richard Allen Kaimann died on January 24, 1999, at the age of 61 years and 3 days.

Four months later, although I was beginning to function again, I was still deeply grieving and trying to adjust to the new "normal" of my life. Aware of time as never before, I knew that a long, empty summer lay before me. What would I do to fill the empty hours, to help the time pass? When the catalogue of summer courses arrived from a nearby college, surprisingly several classes attracted my attention. I signed up for two computer classes and a week-long program in Renaissance art, history, and literature.

Another class caught my eye, a six-week course in creative writing. I tried to ignore it and find some excuse not to enroll. As much as I loved writing on my own—a family history, letters, clever poems for friends' birthdays—I was terrified of a public setting. Could I write on demand? Would I be good enough? Was this the right time, when I was feeling so shaky inside? On the day before the registration deadline, I completed the application.

The computer classes forced me out of the house and increased my skills. Sitting in a computer lab with 20 other people, I shed my identity and my grief. I was a wannabe hack like everyone else. The Renaissance courses delighted and engaged me. I felt transported into another world, outside my sorrow and myself. I had rejoined the world in a non-threatening way.

Then it was time for the writing class. The first evening I was uneasy. The instructor asked the five students why they had enrolled. Most of them wanted to write a novel. Now I was truly intimidated. I confessed, "I'm here because I love to write and I've been putting this off for forty years."

Our first assignment was to develop a character. I wrote "Twenty-One Days" (Chapter 3) about an incident that happened a short time after Dick's death. The next week we read our pieces to the class. I explained that even though my story was written in the third person, it was really about me. As I began reading, I felt my throat constrict and tears well up. I could not continue. I handed the pages to the young woman next to me. As she read, she began to cry. The teacher finished reading the piece. Everyone wept. A long silence followed.

It was those five women who encouraged me to write this book. "You must write your story. People need to read this," said one. "This story is for everyone who has ever had a loss—or ever will."

For the next class I wrote "Dinner for Ten" (Chapter 9), the story of a Saturday evening in May when ten widows gathered for a potluck dinner at my home. Again my classmates encouraged me to continue writing.

From the beginning, when my wound was fresh, I was in awe of the strength and vitality of my widowed friends. Somehow they were able to conduct their lives, work at their jobs, nurture their families, laugh, and have fun. They weren't merely existing. They were truly living. How had they managed to find joy again? Would I ever be able to function so well?

I began to wonder about the common threads that sustain women in the face of great loss. Each situation was unique, but I sensed commonality as well. Each day more questions came to mind: Do people grieve in the same way? Is the impact of a sudden death different from a prolonged one? How do women cope, working their way out of despair? How do our physical bodies respond to grief? How much can we turn to children, family, and friends? How do we face holidays, weddings, and weekends? How do we take over all the responsibilities? Is a support group of value? When do we need professional help? Where do we find spiritual renewal?

My dinner for ten became a springboard for my writing. I asked a few of the women if they would be willing to meet with me and talk about their experiences. To my delight, they said they would.

B'shert is a Yiddish word that means, "It was meant to be." Or by extension, "Everything happens for a reason." I have come to believe that Dick's death was *b'shert*. God had His reasons. *B'shert* does not even whisper that we will ever understand those reasons. Enrolling in the writing class was also *b'shert*.

Each woman's story of loss and recovery has helped me in this difficult process of healing. I have often heard, "When the student is ready, the teacher appears." My friends have been my guides and mentors. I am grateful for their stories and their wisdom.

A friend said to me recently, "You are not the same person you were a year ago. It is as though you have grown wings." I was shocked. Had I really changed? But then, how could anyone not change, when life takes a 180-degree turn? Could I identify those changes, in others and in myself?

In the eight women who have shared their stories, I see an immense reservoir of strength that enables them to lead fulfilling lives. Forged in the crucible of bereavement, this strength has come at a high cost. I would like to think of this strength as a special gift from their husbands.

In addition I believe that they, and I, too, have received a second gift, a gift of the spirit. One of the women told me that when her husband died, a close friend of hers attended the memorial service but did not return to the house afterward. Instead, she called on her later in the evening and explained, "I couldn't come right away. As I was sitting at the service, toward the end, I saw your husband's spirit go into you and each of your children. It was so vivid that I couldn't stay. I had to go home and absorb this experience."

My friend said softly, "This was the most wonderful and comforting gift I could have received on that sad day. It gave me solace then and it gives me solace now."

As I spoke with the women, I came to believe that we are all imbued with the essence of our loved ones. They inspire us, they encourage us, and at times they may even talk to us or guide us. When we allow for this possibility, our own serenity comes more easily.

We who have endured the death of a spouse, who smile and seek purpose and contentment every day, are the women who have embraced these last emotional and spiritual gifts from our husbands as we go about building our new lives. At the beginning we struggled mightily to find some moments of happiness within our overwhelming sadness; over time, we allowed ourselves to experience the inevitable moments of sadness as we moved through our healing.

Somewhere along the way, we all strained very hard and heard a still, small voice, echoing the voices of our husbands as they offered us their final gifts, permission and encouragement to live the most fulfilling lives that we could. We knew we must not let them down.

Thus, even when they are gone, the departed are with us . . .
We remember them now; they live in our hearts; they are an abiding blessing.
—*Gates of Prayer*

Author's Note: On September 11, 2001, shortly after the manuscript for *Common Threads* was completed, hundreds of women suddenly, tragically, shockingly lost their husbands. It is my dearest wish that these stories of women who have walked this difficult path will help the Widows of 9-11 and their families and friends to recognize their own resources and inner strength to rebuild their lives.

Acknowledgments

My special and deepest thanks
To all the people
Who have helped make this book a reality

. . . Eight wonderful women, for sharing their lives with me, for answering my endless questions, and for allowing me to tell their stories.

. . . Rabbi Earl Grollman, for encouraging me time and again, for pointing me in the right direction, and for helping me to think of myself as a writer.

. . . Jack Morgan, for his guidance and motivation.

. . . Cindy Cooper, for the beautiful illustrations.

. . . Paulette Rhoades, for the gift of friendship that saved me, uplifted me, and made me smile through my tears so many times.

. . . Rabbi Francis Barry Silberg, for his deep sensitivity, wisdom, and caring.

. . . Barbara Peltin, for her insights and guidance along the way.

. . . Bill Forman, for his creative ideas, resourcefulness, level head, and constant support.

. . . Holly Bern, Linda Keimel, Lee Raffel, and David Schwartz, for their brilliant editing.

. . . Susan Skibba and the Creative Writing class, who told me I should, said I could, and helped me decide I would write this book.

To the many cherished
Friends and family
Who have been there for me

And finally

. . . Martha and Arthur Schwartz, my dear parents, who always encouraged me and would have been so proud.

Introduction

As an author in the field of death and dying for three decades, I have received many manuscripts from people who have lost a loved one. An accompanying letter usually says, "When my husband/wife/son/daughter/sibling/friend/lover died, I was literally drowning in a sea of sorrow. I have written about my painful feelings and how I was able to survive this terrible ordeal. I am sure that if this were published, countless bereaved people would be helped."

In truth almost every manuscript that I have received contains important observations and precious insights. I truly applaud and encourage these efforts. As someone said, "Writing gets the feelings out of my mind and body and puts them down on paper so I don't feel so alone."

When a dear friend asked if I would look over the draft of a book by a woman who had recently lost her husband, I told him I would. To my great joy, I found Diane Kaimann's *Common Threads* to be a riveting and compelling read. The stories of nine widows' personal journeys are sensitively presented and eminently readable. This book will absorb you, touch you, and will serve as a wellspring of inspiration and consolation. It will be life-enhancing.

When her husband died suddenly in January 1999, Diane Kaimann began a journey that devastated, bewildered, and ultimately inspired and redefined her.

The author's story provides the framework for *Common Threads*. She has interwoven her own saga with vignettes from the lives of eight friends who also faced the deaths of their husbands and the difficult days, months, and years that followed.

The new widow needs a touchstone, an understanding friend who has been there, who comprehends shock and despair, loneliness and fear. In every chapter the survivor will find an emotion, an event, or an issue that is achingly familiar: driving alone, traveling alone, attending a wedding, seeing a rainbow, crying out to a partner who is gone. Moving from one story to the next, the reader hears the voices of nine ordinary yet extraordinary women who have traversed the phases of grief and have gone on to design satisfying lives for themselves.

The reader learns how others have done it—how they rode the roller coaster of feeling better, falling back, going forward again. The women's large and small victories become metaphors for hope and continuity.

Common Threads wraps its arms around the reader and says, "We understand. We know what you are feeling because we have been there. You are not crazy. We embrace you, not just with empathy for your situation, but also with a warm hug and some ideas that will help you on your way—a word, an emotion, an experience you may identify with because you have felt the same way."

The book is not only for the widow but also for all who mourn. It provides valuable insights for family, friends, counselors, clergy, and professionals who want to understand at the most elemental level the struggles and the path of the survivor.

This is an honest book, a book of familiar feelings and experiences—no instruction or preaching here. What an essential source of wisdom, comfort, and hope!

I wholeheartedly recommend *Common Threads* to those who are going through their own grief, and to those who care about them.

Rabbi Earl A. Grollman
D.H.L., D.D.
Author of Living When A Loved One Has Died
Boston, Massachusetts
2001

MISSING YOU

I miss you when the seasons change,
And I recall how you loved the colored leaves,
The first snow, the jonquils, the butterflies,
And working in the yard in your torn Mickey Mouse sweatshirt,
Washing the car, chatting with neighbors.
I miss your scruffy Saturday beard and awful cigars.

I miss you every day and feel your presence
As I walk through the house that you loved and took such pride in.
I miss you when I pass our travel wall of pictures and see you
Kissing a giraffe in Africa,
Trampling the glacier in Canada,
Sitting on a tank in the Golan,
Crunching macadamia nuts in Hawaii,
Always smiling, happy, enjoying wherever you are.

I miss your cantankerous side that would argue over nonsense.
I miss the side that one moment could manufacture mountains out of molehills,
And in the next reduce the most complex issue to simple logic.
I miss your gentle side that loved all cats and stray dogs,
And people who needed your wise counsel.

Your family misses you at holidays.
At Thanksgiving, when we all have dinner together,
We don't understand why you aren't here to slice the turkey
And ask each of us around the table what we are grateful for,
And tell us how much you love each one of us
In a very special way.

We miss your encouragement when we're down,
Your sage suggestions when we're confused,
Your enthusiastic pride when we succeed.

We think of your life
And honor your struggles and your victories,
Your softening and mellowing in recent years.
You gave so much to so many.
We all remember you so vividly.
You are alive to us in so many ways.

Beloved brother, father, uncle, nephew,
Stepfather, brother-in-law, husband —
Dear Dick, we cherish you, we love you —
And most of all, beyond all expressing, we miss you.

Diane and Dick Kaimann on their wedding day, May 15, 1987.

CHAPTER 1

Hawaii, 1999

TEN DAYS IN PARADISE

How does one begin to tell the story of the death of a spouse, a dear husband? I know that as I write this, I will cry and maybe those tears will help me somehow.

In November 1998, Dick and I took a trip to Israel and Jordan. The trip was filled with wonder, learning, and delight. Because we had Frequent Flyer miles expiring, we also planned a trip to Hawaii, a first for us both, from January 14–25, 1999. We would spend three days in Oahu followed by four days on the tiny island of Molokai with Karen and Leonard, Dick's sister and brother-in-law. Then Dick and I would go alone to Maui for four more days.

In Oahu we took a bus tour of Honolulu's many sights and visited Pearl Harbor, where Dick, a history buff, supplemented the guide's information for me. After three days in city traffic, we were happy to leave for the very peaceful island of Molokai. We spent our days and evenings with Karen and Leonard, relaxing, talking, touring, and eating. The most dramatic moment was when I sprained my ankle walking across a golf course.

One day we all visited Purdy's Macadamia Nut Farm, which elicited from us more than one nutty joke. We had fun crushing the nuts in a primitive cracker, and we enjoyed the free samples. We took a very long, harrowing drive along the Halawa coast, with endless hairpin curves and unbelievable views of mountains, rocks, and water. Dick did all the driving, and I closed my eyes a lot.

During those few days, Dick seemed particularly pleased to be with his sister. They were both delighted that we had managed to plan some vacation time together. Because Karen's condo was lacking a coffeepot, each morning Dick would rise early, perk fresh coffee and deliver a large mug to his sister. His eagerness to please her was endearing.

On January 21, we celebrated Dick's 61st birthday and Karen and Leonard's 37th anniversary at a lovely restaurant on the beach. Before we ate, we joined the crowd watching a spectacular sunset. As the sun appeared to slip into the ocean and the sky changed from bright orange to misty darkness, Dick clicked away with his camera. Then we adjourned to the dining room.

Karen said, "It just doesn't get any better than this." We all agreed.

As a young man, Dick was an excellent and enthusiastic athlete. In his forties, he discovered scuba diving. He took many courses and became certified as an advanced open-water diver by the Professional Association of Diving Instructors. He logged hundreds of hours of diving experience in Lake Michigan, the Cayman Islands, the Truk Islands in the South Pacific, and the Red Sea. He loved the challenge and adventure of entering the silent world beneath the sea, seeing the magnificent and amazing fish and plants. He found scuba diving relaxing and invigorating.

Dick was excited about diving in Hawaii. Before leaving home, he made arrangements to go diving in Molokai, but when we arrived, the dive guide announced that he was not available. Dick was disappointed. Two days later the guide called and was able to offer Dick a diving time for our last day on the island.

Afterwards Dick mentioned that it was not a great dive because the water was too cold and there wasn't much to see, but I could tell that he was still pleased that he had gone. Later that evening, he said, "I have a twinge in my chest."

"You often have twinges," I offered.

"I know," he said, "but this one is different." I can't recall his mentioning the twinge again. I was more concerned with my throbbing ankle.

In December of 1986, six months before we were married, Dick had undergone six arterial bypasses. His recovery was good. In 1993 he had a minor heart attack followed by angioplasty. Again he recovered well, attended his cardiac rehab program regularly, and usually watched his diet. Dick's cardiologist considered the discomfort in one area of his chest a perfectly normal result of the surgery.

I often questioned whether a person with a heart condition should go scuba diving. What would he do if he had chest pain under water? He could not lie down, take a nitroglycerin pill, or call for help. I would ask, "Dick, what do your doctors say?" Dick would tell the doctor how relaxing the diving was for him, how good he felt in the water. Their response? According to Dick, while the doctors tried to discourage him, they did not go so far as to forbid it. Since his surgery, Dick had taken several major dive trips. The diving had presented no problems.

On Thursday morning we said good-bye to Karen and Leonard, who would be returning to Milwaukee the next day. We left for Maui, Dick hauling all his heavy dive gear and complaining about my luggage. We rented a car and drove to Wailea, a beautiful area, very quiet and elegant, and checked into our hotel.

The room assigned to us was practically below ground level, and Dick groused. He seemed unduly upset about this, so I called the front desk and requested a room change, which was promised for the next day. Then I turned on the TV, watched a video of all the restaurants on Maui, and jotted down a list of suggestions for dinners and activities I thought we would enjoy.

The first night we attended a luau at the hotel. The next morning we signed up for a plane trip on Sunday evening, our last night in Hawaii. We would fly over the Big Island and see active volcanoes. We agreed that this would be far more exciting than a long drive through mountains to see defunct craters with no fire.

Happier now, in a sunny room with a lovely view of the ocean, we went down to sit in the whirlpool before dinner. That evening we enjoyed one of our finest meals ever. When we walked into the restaurant, Dick looked around, grinned and said, "Now this is our kind of place."

And it was—low-key, casual, with a large open grill. Our waiter made excellent suggestions. The salad and tapenade were so delicious that I requested recipes. Because I am a vegetarian, Dick and I rarely chose the same foods. I cannot remember any other time when we ordered dishes to split. But that evening we shared hors d'ouevres, salad, and entrée. Then we decided to splurge on a rich dessert, vanilla ice cream drizzled with melted chocolate and crumbled macadamia nuts—delicious! We were full and happy.

On Saturday morning we attended a time-share presentation and saw a lovely condo. I became enthusiastic. We learned that if you own a time-share on Maui, you have "Maui Power"—negotiable for any vacation, any time, any place. I was hooked and would have left a deposit on the spot. But Dick, more cautious and more resistant to sales pressure, was nowhere near ready. He told me he would research this further when we got home.

After viewing the condo, we toured a tropical plantation, where we saw how the flowers and fruit are raised on the islands. Then we drove to Lahaina, an old whaling village set along what seemed like one endless, sparkling green golf course. We decided to sign up for an afternoon whale-watching trip and, since we had a little time, we went to visit the Whalers Museum, which reminded Dick of diving and me of *Moby Dick*. During lunch Dick seemed a little tired, so I didn't press him to go into the tempting boutiques.

With still an hour to wait for the whaling trip, we sat under the famous and amazing banyan tree. The branches have sprouted numerous trunks that have grown down into the soil so that this single tree covers a large park in the center of town. We watched tourists taking pictures of each other in front of the tree. Finally, we boarded the whale-watching boat. As we left the dock, we saw a large cruise ship, the *Queen Elizabeth II*. This turned out to be our best sighting of the day because apparently the whales were on a trip of their own. The boat ride was pleasant and made us ravenous.

Our dinner at Roy's more than made up for the whale disappointment. Again we had a wonderful meal, and again we shared, course by course. "This is a good idea," Dick said. "What made you think about sharing?"

"I thought we could each taste more different foods," I told him.

Every course was special, but the dessert, a chocolate puff pastry filled with hot fudge and doused with whipped cream, was spectacular. Once more we were sated and pleased with our choice of restaurant and menu.

Back in the room, I went to bed while Dick sat on the balcony, reading and smoking a cigar. When he came to bed, the aroma came with him.

LAST DAY IN PARADISE

After his chilly dive in Molokai, Dick said that he probably would not dive in Maui. On Sunday morning, he told me he was taking his book down to the pool to read and suggested I join him when I was ready. A few minutes later he returned to the room, all smiles, obviously excited.

"Guess what—I'm going diving. They tell me the water is warm." He changed into his wet suit and left for the dive shop.

With time to myself, I decided to take a walk along Hotel Row. I went downstairs and out the main door. Standing near the driveway was a young bellman, whose nametag identified him as Curtis. I asked him about the best route for someone with a sprained ankle. He suggested that I walk to the main road and then take the bus, which would stop at each hotel.

As I was about to leave, he said, "You know, you might just want to take the path along the beach. Lots of people walk there, and it's a much prettier view." That sounded better, so I went back through the hotel and started down toward the path, which led past the dive shop.

There was Dick, standing by the shop's entrance, in his bright yellow and black dive suit. "Are you coming or going?" I asked.

"We're just about ready to start."

Dick, a dive guide, another man, and a young woman comprised the group.

"If I had thought about it, I could have brought the camera and taken your picture," I said. The divers were ready to go, so I called out to Dick, "Have a fun time."

Dick pointed to a nearby beach chair, "My stuff is over there. See you in a bit."

I watched the divers head down an inclined path, maybe a hundred feet, toward the beach. It seemed a long way to carry all that heavy gear. I walked toward my path, looked over and saw the divers standing in the water. I blinked once and in that split second, they had all disappeared under the waves.

My walk lasted probably an hour and a half. I wandered into a few spectacular hotels and was amazed. Many people refer to Hawaii as Paradise—and for good reason. Every view delights the eye. From the canopies of the trees comes a constant cacophony of bird songs. The flowers are enormous, the air is perfumed, and the temperature is moderate. The sea is the bluest blue; the lava along the shore is the blackest black. The mountains seem happy just to be there, as do the people, who are friendly and helpful. I felt relaxed as I continued my solitary walk, anticipating a restful day, the adventurous plane ride, and maybe another grand dinner.

On my return walk, I met a couple we had seen on Molokai. The woman had just learned that her mother, aged 90, had died in Holland, and she felt so far away. I was struck at the thought of death in such a beautiful setting. It seemed incongruous. Did I shudder or recoil? Maybe. We chatted for at least fifteen minutes. By then I was anxious to be on my way; Dick would be wondering where I was.

As I neared the hotel, I saw several police cars huddled in a small parking area near the beach. Suddenly a woman in a dive suit pulled away from a crowd of bystanders. She was the woman from the dive group. She walked rapidly toward me.

"Aren't you Dick's wife?" When I said yes, she reached out and took my hand. She said quietly, "Something has happened." A shiver of apprehension whipped through me.

Then she drew me toward a policeman, while explaining to me that Dick had had a problem coming up after the dive, that an ambulance had arrived to take him to the hospital. I shivered again, harder.

A policeman with a note pad started asking me questions, mostly about Dick's medical history. The woman diver, who was growing impatient, finally said forcefully to him, "This woman needs to go to the hospital right now to be with her husband."

Someone from the hotel said that a car was coming to drive me. While we waited, I knew that this was serious. The woman handed me a tiny piece of paper with her name and phone number. Julie. She asked that I call and let her know how things went. Finally a car arrived, driven by Curtis, whom I recognized. Paul, a pleasant, dark-haired young man who also worked at the hotel, accompanied us.

The ride seemed endless, probably thirty minutes, and the two men conversed quietly. Curtis talked about his trip to the ER earlier in the week when a falling ceiling fan hit his little boy on the head. At some point on the drive, after what felt like hours to me, I looked at the digital clock. 12:46. Curtis told me we were about halfway there. I tried to will the car to move faster. I was frightened. I tried to pray. I couldn't.

When we arrived at the hospital, Paul volunteered to go in with me. He was tall and strong and kind, and I was grateful for his offer. The reception area was empty. After that long, terrible drive, no one was there to direct us. Finally, after several minutes, a woman appeared and ushered us into a small conference room where I sat down at a table. Paul stood behind me. The woman said, "I need to ask you some questions."

"And I need to ask you a question—how is my husband?" By now I was scared and impatient.

"The doctor will be in shortly to talk to you. What is your husband's social security number?"

"I haven't the vaguest idea," I mumbled, annoyed.

"What religion are you?"

"Jewish."

A doctor appeared in the room. Paul put his hand on my shoulder. When I tried to stand, the doctor moved his hands, indicating that I should sit down.

"Please sit," he said. "I'm afraid I don't have good news." I thought to myself, Dick must be very sick and they are treating him.

The doctor continued gently. "We did all we could, but we couldn't save him. Your husband died."

I froze. Then, I heard a long, high wail—coming from me.

Behind me, Paul, still holding my shoulder, began to cry.

After I had quieted somewhat, the doctor explained that Dick had received CPR in the ambulance and that the doctors had worked on him for forty minutes in the ER, but they were never able to get an electrical impulse. His heart would not beat on its own. For some reason I asked about the time of death: 12:43.

The doctor said what he could to comfort me, and then began talking about the medical examiner. What did he mean?

Minutes passed. I asked someone if I could see Dick. Yes, he was in a room down the hall. I stepped into the hallway and turned. Suddenly the doctor reappeared and asked where I was going.

When I told him, he put a hand on my shoulder and said, "Diane, Dick is not here. You are here, but he is not. I don't think you want to see him. Remember him the way he was." He guided me back into a reception room. I was never asked to identify my husband.

Someone asked if there was anything he could do for me. I asked for Dick's watch, which he always wore. Someone brought it to me. I asked if there was a rabbi on the island. Someone left the room to find out. Then I asked for a phone. I was directed to a pay phone outside the building. My shaking fingers struggled to find coins and to press the buttons.

First I tried to call Dick's sister Karen, but the call would not go through so I called my son Bruce and his wife Jodi in New York. When Jodi answered, I blurted out what had happened. I could hear the shock and disbelief.

Bruce picked up the phone and cried out, "Mom—Oh, NOOO." Collecting himself, he said he would call the rest of the family.

Someone told me that I must wait to talk with the assistant medical examiner that had been called. By then I was on autopilot and simply accepted that this was what I had to do. Minutes or hours passed while we waited. Three very kind Jewish people working in the hospital came to be with me. Then the president of the Temple in Kihei, near Wailea, called and told me of a couple who could come to the hotel if I would like. Yes, please.

I received two phone calls on the hospital pay phone, one from Karen and one from my daughter Margie. Their shock reverberated all the way from Milwaukee. They both asked what I would do now. I didn't know.

Finally the assistant medical examiner arrived. When he explained that they might need to do an autopsy, I gasped and said, "*Please, no.*"

He explained that in Hawaii every sudden death requires an autopsy, but he couldn't say for certain how the coroner would rule.

"Please, no cutting."

Unmoved, the man said that the coroner would consider the circumstances and make the final decision about the autopsy. They would be in touch with me sometime next week.

Final decision? Next week? Sometime? What was this foreign language? Hot anger burned into my shocked brain.

From the back of my mind, two thoughts emerged: some Jews consider an autopsy a desecration of the human body; also, a funeral is to be held as soon as possible, so that the soul can rest and the survivors can begin their official mourning.

My husband had died, and the State of Hawaii was making the decisions. I was too drained to protest further. I was so beside myself that I had to leave the hospital or I would cave in. But how could I leave Dick there, all alone in the hospital? I shuddered to think of where he would spend the next hours or days. But he wouldn't know because he was dead. *Dead? No!* The doctors would revive him and we would fly home together tomorrow as planned. I was having a nightmare. Soon I would wake up.

Finally we were allowed to leave for the long, terrible, beautiful ride back to the hotel. I asked Paul, who had a cell phone, to call ahead to the hotel and request that someone cancel our plans for the evening and also to arrange for me to meet with Carlos, the dive guide. I wanted to explain Dick's medical history to him.

As we rode back, the thought of spending more hours on this island, in our room, became unbearable. If this really was happening and not a nightmare, then I couldn't wait until our scheduled flight on Monday. I had to leave this place immediately. I had to be with my family. What I would have given to be magically transported home.

Please, could I be on a flight home tonight?

By the time we arrived at the hotel, arrangements were in place for someone to take me to the airport later in the afternoon for the flight to Honolulu, and then for me to fly back home.

Quietly, Paul asked if I would like him to come to the room with me. Yes. I couldn't face that room alone. Paul had become my support. But, of course, he wouldn't need to stay long because Dick would be back any minute from his dive trip.

I had to strain to bring myself back to reality.

In our hotel room I tried to complete the mechanical tasks I knew I must do: pack, shower, and dress for the trip. Paul helped me with Dick's clothes. I didn't know if I could do that alone.

Phone calls began to come in, one after another: my brother David and his wife Anne from Virginia; dear friends from Chicago; our rabbi and his wife; Dick's son Fred from New Jersey, who volunteered to come out and fly home with me. Everyone was in shock about Dick, and they were also concerned that I had to go through this alone, and that I was so far from home.

As I spoke to each person, I heard a voice that was mine—numb, controlled. I tried to assure all of them that I would be able to travel home alone, even though I had my doubts.

A knock at the door. The Meyers, a lovely couple, and their friend Barbara, from the Kihei congregation entered the room. The two women helped me pack my suitcase. They were so dear and caring. I was a total stranger to them, but in those moments they took the place of my family, and I was thankful for their presence and their help. We talked for a short while, they hugged me, wished me well, and left.

Two minutes later, Carlos arrived still in his dive suit. He told me from his perspective what had happened. At the end of the dive, Dick had given the thumbs up sign, which for divers means, "I know the dive is over. I'm ready to go up."

According to Carlos, the group began swimming toward shore. Carlos said that he was the first one out of the water. When he became aware that Dick was in trouble, he swam back out and saw that Dick was not conscious. Carlos tore off his weight belt and Dick's and then began pulling him to shore. On the beach a crowd had gathered. Two nurses and a doctor who were on the scene started CPR.

After Carlos left, Paul hugged me good-bye. Suddenly I was alone, with no kindly strangers. I wished I had said to the Meyers, "Please don't leave me alone." It felt eerie to be in the room where Dick and I had spent several happy days. I was afraid to be by myself.

Then I realized how little time there was before my ride to the airport. I took a shower and dressed. I had been alone for twenty minutes and had survived. Even in my shock, I felt a tiny victory. I had taken the first baby step.

The phone rang again. It was Julie, the diver. Would I like her to come by? As overwhelmed as I was with preparing to leave, I knew that seeing her was important. She was likely the last person who had seen Dick alive. "Yes, please come over."

Julie told me about the beautiful dive. They heard whales and saw lovely fish and innumerable sea turtles. She told me that Dick had been most solicitous of her as a novice diver, and she appreciated his kindness and encouragement. Drinking in every word, I felt the tears welling as I thought how thrilled Dick must have been to see those fish and turtles, and how excited he would have been to describe them to me in colorful detail.

Dick was last in line swimming toward shore, perhaps because he was the most experienced diver. Julie was ahead of Dick. The last time she looked back, he was swimming in behind her. When she had almost reached the shore, she turned around and didn't see Dick. She called out to the guide, "Where's Dick?"

Then she saw him floating some distance out and thought he was just playing. She saw one foot move—a kick or a wave? Julie wasn't sure. A little more time elapsed. When she looked again, she realized that Dick had not moved at all. She yelled for the guide, who then swam out. Other people came and helped. She had no real idea of the elapsed time. She did say that Dick's color was "not right." She thought perhaps he regained some color once on shore, but he had lost that by the time the ambulance arrived many minutes later.

I thanked her for coming. She told me she was a family law attorney in Washington, D.C. She gave me her office and home numbers and promised to be in touch.

The longest day and night of my life were just beginning.

GOING HOME

God has a habit of placing in your path exactly the foothold you need at that moment.

—Maimonides

Somehow I made myself function, and by 5 o'clock I was on my way to the airport, almost composed. I prayed, "Dear God, please be with Dick. And I know this long trip home will be terrible. Please help me through it."

The driver stayed with me until I was on the plane. I was able to check my bags through from Maui. In order to have the seating that we had paid for in business class, I was changed to a flight with a stop in Memphis instead of Minneapolis. While I was waiting in line to board, I heard myself being paged. I raised my hand. A moment later a police officer was standing beside me, asking me the same questions I had been asked half a day ago near the beach.

I had once read that when one has a severe shock, it is like a sharp blade that cuts into you so cleanly and with such force that you may not feel the pain until a while later. That is exactly how I felt, cut but numb. All I wanted was to go home.

On the small plane from Maui to Honolulu, my eyes were wet. With people sitting so close to me, I didn't want to cry aloud and draw attention to myself. As the plane lifted into the air, I started to feel like a bad wife. Was I abandoning Dick, leaving him alone in Hawaii? Should I have waited with him until he could fly back with me?

Exhausted, I closed my eyes. The hum of the engine lulled me. I must have dozed off for a moment, and in that state I could almost believe that Dick and I were on the little plane to the Big Island, where we would see erupting volcanoes. When I woke up, I remembered that something was terribly wrong.

When we landed, I misunderstood directions to the Northwest terminal and took the wrong airport shuttle. After wandering around in the twilight, I finally connected with the right shuttle to my terminal. On this warm Sunday night, the entire airport was dimly lit and almost empty of travelers. Finally I found the waiting room, a huge, cavernous hall with a high ceiling. From where I was standing in the doorway, the waiting area appeared to be a converted airplane hangar. Night had fallen, filling the space with darkness. I felt as if I were in a surreal dream.

I looked at my watch; I would have a four-hour wait, alone. The thought of being by myself for so many hours terrified me. I very much needed to talk to someone. My eyes canvassed the empty hall. Far to the left was a woman sitting alone, reading a book.

I rolled my carry-on toward her and sat down two seats away. I looked into the face of a woman who appeared to be in her mid-fifties, with long, reddish hair, kind eyes, and a gentle smile. I asked, "May I talk to you?"

"Of course," she said.

The words spilled out. "My husband died today and I'm on my way home." I burst into tears.

Immediately, the woman stood up, came over to me, and then held me in her arms. When I tried to apologize for my outburst, she said, "Please don't even think about it. For some reason, I am the person that people come to when they are troubled. My name is Paulette."

In that moment, I sensed that I could trust this woman to give me the comfort I needed so desperately. I clung to her kindness and to the hope for some relief from my anguish.

Finally my weeping diminished and our friendship began. As women do, even at the most emotional moments, we began to talk about our lives and ourselves. Paulette had been vacationing in Maui with her daughter and son-in-law. When she told them she wanted to be alone to read her book, they went for a walk. I expressed concern that I was keeping her from her family, but she assured me that after a week of togetherness, it was fine.

Paulette let me talk for a while. It was as though we were destined to be friends, and we needed to exchange our histories in capsule form so that we could go forward. Then she asked if I had eaten. I vaguely remembered nibbling at a cheese sandwich. We wandered the dark corridors of the airport until we found food. As we talked over a bowl of Korean soup, I learned that my new friend had recently retired from a career with the telephone company. She told me that she was embarking upon a new dual career, hypnotherapy and medical massage.

In spite of my grief, I was able to tell her about my own career history, first as a teacher, then as a business owner for many years, and about my current work as a consultant to women entrepreneurs. Suddenly, I found my brain switching to another channel, and I started to give her some ideas on how to launch her new business. She was interested and attentive. I explained that Dick was a business consultant and that was how I had become involved in consulting.

Then she asked me about Dick. I found myself trying to sum up my husband's life for a person who would never know him. I told her that he had grown up in Milwaukee and graduated from Rensselaer Polytechnic Institute in Troy, New York, in 1960. He had wanted to become an astronaut, but he was severely injured when he was slapped across the back with a hockey stick during a college game. After that he changed his major to computers and management engineering. Later he earned an MBA from Marquette University.

In 1964 he started his own consulting business, specializing in computer applications in business. In 1967, Dick received a doctorate from the University of Iowa in computer science. For the next twenty years, he was a professor of information systems and operations management at Marquette University. After he stopped teaching, he turned his full attention to his consulting practice.

Paulette and I returned to the waiting room, where we continued talking with the ease of two old friends. I told her in more detail about the horrible day and about how kind people had been to me. She was quiet for a moment, as though debating whether to speak. Finally she said, "I'm going to tell you something, and if you're not interested, that's fine. Do you know what psychometry is?"

I shook my head. She explained that she had a particular gift. She told me a story about a young man in her town who had committed suicide. Knowing of her gift and distraught by the man's death, his family approached Paulette. She asked for an object that had belonged to the man. As she held it, she conveyed information that she had no way of knowing. She enumerated several details concerning the man. His family was comforted and appreciative.

Then she stopped talking. I looked into her earnest face. Did I believe such things were possible? Did I want to? If I was looking for a trace of deceit in Paulette's face, I saw only compassion. She was offering to help me.

On this strangest and most terrible of days, what did I have to lose? I was desperate, desperate to reach out somehow to Dick, to have one more communication. I wanted Paulette to bring my husband to me in whatever way she could. If I was grasping at straws, straining for consolation, so what?

I told myself that probably nothing would come of this, even as I dug through my purse and pulled out the plastic baggie holding Dick's watch. Grains of sand stuck to the metal. I held out the watch to Paulette.

"Would you do that for me?" I asked.

"I will try," she answered.

As she held the watch, I could hardly look at her. After a minute or two, she smiled and spoke softly.

"What I hear is, 'I'm home, gal . . . and I have so much to do.'"

Tears filled my eyes, and I almost smiled.

Paulette continued slowly, "I have the feeling he is very happy, and he's kind of scurrying around in this new place. He's very busy." Pause. "He loved you so much. He thought you were beautiful inside and out." Another pause. "He left very quickly, almost in an instant, without suffering." Another pause. "Your Mom says 'hello.'" She was silent for almost a minute. "I feel that Dick is on a new path, a highly spiritual path, and this is all very new to him. He is amazed. There is so much he never knew. I sense a lightness. It's as though he is enraptured." Paulette stopped again for a moment. "He left because he has new things to learn. He's so busy with all the wonder that he doesn't realize yet that he's left you alone. I see old men with beards, singing or chanting, welcoming him. They seem happy to greet him, glad he is there."

I could barely speak. "It sounds like he is happy," I managed to say through my tears. For an instant I actually felt some relief.

"Very happy."

We sat silently. Then Paulette handed me the watch. The metal band was hot. "That is the energy coming through." She told me she had chills on her arm, and that this was confirmation for her that she was really in touch with Dick.

After a moment I asked Paulette if she was afraid of death.

"Not at all."

I wanted her to tell me more about Dick. "Do you get more?"

She answered slowly, "He's going to be watching over you very closely for a while. Whenever you feel very warm or flushed, he is there with you."

All through this, I listened and wept and held on tightly to every syllable. I knew I must remember every word. I wanted to hear more, but this was all she had. Her words calmed me.

People began filing into the airport. When I realized that Paulette and I would be taking the same flight to San Francisco, I tried to arrange for her to sit with me in business class. Tearfully, I explained the situation to the ticket agent, who was sympathetic but explained that he did not have two seats together in business class. However, he suggested that if I wanted to fly from San Francisco to Minneapolis with Paulette, he could put me back on the Minneapolis flight and arrange for us to sit together in coach.

At first I didn't want to give up the comfort of business class. Then my instincts told me that I needed Paulette's comfort more than I needed extra legroom. Just before we boarded, the agent came over to say that two seats together had opened up in business class on the San Francisco flight. For that moment I was happy and relieved.

As we boarded the plane and prepared for the flight, I realized that I was uncharacteristically relaxed about flying. I didn't really care what might happen. If the plane crashed, then I would be with Dick. Despite my exhaustion and a sleeping pill from the hotel doctor, I couldn't sleep. All night I was awake and crying. When I had a bad spell, Paulette held me and stroked my hair. It was a long night.

The next day, on the flight to Minneapolis, I said to Paulette, "I have Dick's ticket case with me. Would you try again?"

"Of course."

After a few seconds, she said, "He's going to look out for your daughter, and he is getting lots of help from the old men."

"You mean he'll be like her guardian angel?" I asked.

"Yes. And he's saving a place for you."

"Not too soon, I hope."

Then Paulette asked a curious question, "What was Dick's father like?"

His father had died before I met Dick, so I tried to tell her what little I knew, that he was short, stocky, and a little gruff. "Why did you ask?"

"I see an older man, rather slight, slim, a very gentle man."

I felt a chill, then a warm feeling. "That's *my* dad."

Do I believe in miracles? Answers to prayer? Guardian spirits? I'm not sure, but I do know that on that day, in my yearning to have a few more moments with Dick, I suspended disbelief and accepted what Paulette told me. I wanted to know that Dick still existed somewhere and that he was okay. How soothing Paulette's words were for me.

A few years ago I read two of Shirley MacLaine's books, as well as some books on near death experiences. Although I was intrigued, I have never considered myself particularly spiritual, and definitely not psychic or New Age. But even so, I find hope in a line from *Hamlet*: "There are more things in heaven and earth, Horatio, than are dreamed of in your philosophy."

In poetry, water is often symbolic of birth and death. Before I even met Dick, he had sent me a photograph of himself, underwater, in his dive suit and mask. I couldn't see his face very well. My last sight of Dick was in his dive suit and mask, going under water. Alpha and omega.

Certainly, Hawaii is Paradise on earth. The last place Dick saw was this Paradise. In his last few days of life, he enjoyed every sense. He died doing what he loved best, with the fish and his beloved sea around him.

I think of the woman I had met on the walking path. While I was hearing about her mother's death, I was spared witnessing my husband's. Had I not stopped to talk with her, I might have arrived back in time to see the commotion on the beach. I was protected from terrible memories.

Two days after my return, I had some time to talk with Dick's oldest and dearest friend, Howard, who is a very spiritual person. He said that he thought he knew what had happened to Dick.

"You do?" I asked, astounded.

He said, "Do you know anything about dolphins?"

"Not really. Only that they talk to each other."

Howard nodded. "That's true. They are intelligent, but they also are very spiritual creatures, in many traditions and over all of time. When Dick was in the water, the dolphins came to him and said, 'It's time to go.' Dick answered them, 'But I'm not ready. I haven't said good-bye to my wife and family.'"

"'Well,' said the dolphins, 'You have two choices. We can send you back, but you will be a very sick man. It will be very hard on you and very hard on your family. You'll be in the hospital on respirators and machines. Soon you will die. Or we can take your spirit now and spare you and your family much pain. We will leave your body because your family will need that. What is your choice?'"

Howard paused, then said softly, "Dick decided to spare you and everyone else, and he went with the dolphins."

I think of this story often. I know that this is the choice Dick would have made.

Several months later, my dear friend Nancy, with whom I had shared this story, gave me a birthday gift. I opened the small, rectangular box. Inside was a red velvet cloth, which I lifted carefully. Resting on its side was a beautiful, translucent crystal dolphin.

GOOD-BYE, SWEETHEART

I arrived home on Monday afternoon, exhausted but glad to be embraced by Margie and Karen. At last I was not alone in my suffering. The day was cold and bleak; the drive home from the airport was long and silent because none of us could speak. What was there to say?

When I stepped from the car, my legs nearly gave way. How could I be coming home from Hawaii without Dick? I stumbled through the house and collapsed on the bed. All I wanted was rest. I took a sleeping pill and entered a dark, dreamless slumber. I woke up, looked over for Dick, and cried.

By evening, family and friends filled the house in an outpouring of kindness. The phone rang day and night. Leslie, a close friend, masterminded preparations for large amounts of food for feeding all the people who came by to convey their condolences.

On Tuesday, the people from out of town started to arrive: Fred, Bruce and Jodi; my brother David, his wife Anne, and their two daughters; Karen and Leonard's four children. We all wept together, held each other, and shared meals and memories.

At Fred's suggestion, we set out old and more recent photos of his father. He thought that people would enjoy their reminiscences of Dick. After our trip to Israel and Jordan, I had assembled a picture album. Because we had been with a group of eager photographers, we were able to bring back many pictures of Dick and me together. When gathering photos to display for our guests, I could not find that particular album. Frantic, I tore apart closets, emptied shelves. Not being able to locate the pictures added to my distress.

At times I was able to converse. I welcomed every hug, every shared tear or "Dick" story—and there were so many—some of them told by friends who had known him in grade school and high school. I kept hoping that each new visitor would make me feel better, that this would be the person who could ease my pain. No one could. Dick was not there. Surely our host would arrive any minute to greet each of his guests, make some witty comment, enjoy the delicious food, and tell everyone about the sea turtles. Then, with a jolt, the truth would hit me again, and I would have to walk away.

On Wednesday, Barry Silberg, our rabbi and longtime friend, came to meet with me. He offered what comfort he could, and then listened as I shared with him four pages of anecdotes and perceptions about Dick. The rabbi hugged me and left with my notes.

The days were like one long day to me. I went to bed, I woke up. I never left the house. It was only at home that I felt safe. At night I sweated profusely. Shock? Jet lag? My agony was nearly unbearable. My sorrow was not yet for me, but for the rest of Dick's life that he would never have. I missed seeing his tan, masculine face, his strong, thick hands, and his dark brown, intelligent eyes. I ached to hear his deep voice and to feel his presence in the house. I had never felt such pain.

Compounding the anguish of that week were the logistics of death. The funeral director communicated with the medical examiner in Hawaii, who had determined that an autopsy must be performed. Until the police released the body, we could not set a day for the funeral. *The body?* This was my husband, Fred's dad, Karen's brother—not *the body.*

The funeral director telephoned two or three times a day about the arrangements. While he was kind and tactful, these conversations were very painful. The uncertainty about when Dick would be returned from Hawaii brought all of us additional angst. Moreover, our religious traditions and preferences were disregarded, specifically in the matters of the autopsy and the timing for the burial. We were too far away to be effective in our protestations. To the State of Hawaii, we were voices on a phone thousands of miles away.

Late Wednesday, we learned that the autopsy was complete and that a flight had been arranged for Thursday. I blocked the mental images of these proceedings. At last we were able to set the funeral for Friday, January 29th at 11 in the morning. That settled, next came the terrible task of going to the mortuary and selecting a casket. When Karen and Fred offered to go in my stead, I was deeply relieved. I simply did not have the strength.

Finally it was Friday. The day was clear and cold. After breakfast, I returned to my bedroom to dress. I reached out to the spot on the dresser where I kept my wedding band. It wasn't there. Distraught, I swept off the top of the dresser with my hand, hoping the ring was underneath a tissue or a scarf. No ring. I checked the entire room. I crawled around on the floor, brushing my hand over yards of carpet. Still no ring. How could I go to my husband's funeral without my wedding band? I had no choice. I put on my black suit and combed my hair.

Relatives, friends, colleagues, clients, and admirers of Dick filled the funeral home. Earlier, Karen and I had agreed that we would forego a receiving line before the service. We both knew we could not bear to shake all the hands and hear all the words that could not ease our pain. Standing and talking would be too much of a strain. Fortunately, the funeral home arranged for family members to sit alone, in a separate room. As I looked out into the main chapel, I saw the casket for the first time. I collapsed into the nearest chair.

Soon the service began. From the other room I could hear prayers in Hebrew and English. Then the rabbi began his eulogy. As I watched and listened, I recognized that he had taken my notes and turned them into poignant poetry. As he delivered the eloquent words, his rich, full voice and his expressive eyes conveyed his deep sorrow for us. As he spoke, he looked toward me many times.

The fifteen-minute ride from the funeral home to the cemetery seemed endless. The hearse drove in front of us, but I couldn't look. I closed my eyes for the entire trip and wept silently.

At the cemetery we trudged up a narrow path through the snow to the gravesite. The family sat under a canopy, facing a large, gaping hole in the earth. Suspended above it was the casket. I could not grasp the idea that my husband was inside.

When we rose for the burial prayers, my children stood on either side of me, with their arms around my shoulders. Then it was time to lower the casket. The rudimentary mechanism creaked and groaned, as if resisting its harsh work. The two gravediggers, in their overalls and plaid caps, seemed indifferent and clumsy. At last, when I thought I would scream if this work went on one more moment, the casket clanked its way to the bottom.

In keeping with Jewish tradition, the mourners—family and friends— approached the hole one at a time, picked up a shovel resting there, scooped dirt from a mound next to the opening, and dropped it into the grave. Dozens of people stepped forward. Slowly, the dirt began to fill the space around and over the casket. Each time some dirt hit the casket, the sound reverberated in my heart.

I knew then that Dick really had died. We were burying my husband.

The rabbi nodded for me to take my turn. My hands and legs shook. I lifted the heavy shovel, dug a handful of dirt from the pile, dropped it slowly onto my husband's casket, and whispered softly, "Good-bye, sweetheart."

CHAPTER 2

A Gift of Apricots

In the days and weeks after the funeral, many visitors came by. Some were close friends; others were people who had known Dick in the various avenues of his life and wanted to pay their respects. Although I always appreciated the kind words and was usually glad for the company, it was stressful to meet new people at that time.

When Sara Sanders came to see me about two weeks after Dick's funeral, I knew almost nothing about her. We had only met once or twice. I recalled that she had gone to high school with Dick, that she was a widow. When Sara called and asked to come by, I wondered if I was up to making small talk with someone I barely knew. Would I have the energy? She sounded so kind. How could I turn away from a hand extended?

A little while later Sara arrived, clambering easily over the snowdrifts on the front walk. She pulled off her boots and handed me a bag of apricots—how did she know that I love apricots? In the middle of winter, apricots are a promise of warmer and sunnier days. We sat down. With no prologue, Sara looked me directly in the eye and asked, "How *ARE* you? How are you doing?"

I blinked. Did she really want to hear? From the tone of her voice, I knew that her questions were genuine. She would listen with her heart. She waited silently for me to reply in my own words, not trying to fill space with hers.

And so I told her. When I finished, Sara said to me, "I can only share with you what I went through and I can only hope it will help you in the smallest way." Then Sara told me about herself.

To view the many dimensions of Sara Sanders, you need to put on your track shoes, chase after her awhile, and observe what she's wearing because her persona changes in any given day with her wardrobe. When you meet Sara, you admire her petite, athletic build, short curly brown hair, and her dainty face dusted with tiny freckles. She wears round, wire-framed glasses. Her fresh, youthful appearance allows her the luxury of employing a minimum of makeup. In short, Sara is cute, an adjective usually past its prime for women in their mid-fifties. As you chug along with Sara through her hectic day, you admire this active, competent, confident woman.

If you're out at 5 A.M. to enjoy a shiny summer morning, or a sparkling winter one, you'll see Sara in her running outfit, shorts or sweats, sweatband or knitted hat. Sara denies that she is obsessed with running, but her regimen of four miles on weekdays, eight on weekends, 52 weeks a year hints at more than a passing interest in the sport.

When she injured her foot, Sara made the rounds of doctors until she found one who understood the importance of her running and permitted her to continue on a limited basis. She cut back to a mere three and seven miles. When she talked about running, a look of absolute exultation burst across her face.

By 8 A.M. Sara has showered and is dressed in a navy suit, white blouse and comfortable heels, ready to leave on the 30-minute commute to her office. Come on Saturday evening and you'll find Sara in her favorite dress-up outfit: khakis, a brown knit T-shirt, and a matching cropped sweater tossed over her shoulders. A mutual friend jokingly said to me, "Looking at Sara is almost enough to make me consider running."

Always interested in medicine, Sara trained as a nurse and started her career in 1962 in public health, working in the inner city for three years. Her job duties included being a school nurse in two schools, teaching well-baby clinics, and visiting families with community health problems like tuberculosis. When her own children were born, Sara stayed home for 18 years, returning to work in 1983. She worked as an occupational health nurse for the post office for a year and a half.

For the last fourteen years, Sara has worked for a company engaged by insurance companies and the Federal government to make certain that employees who are on Workers' Compensation receive the best care. The ultimate goal is to enable workers to return to work. Sara and the seven nurses whom she supervises have their own caseloads and serve as liaisons between patient, employer, and medical professionals.

Rarely have I heard anyone speak so positively about every aspect of her job. Sara especially values the variety, which may include analyzing a worker's specific tasks or videotaping the work environment. She sees many cases of carpal tunnel syndrome, back injury, stress, and post-traumatic stress syndrome.

"My work is stimulating, interesting, challenging. It is also a fabulous job. I have autonomy and flexibility. Very few people have the kind of job I have. There are 25 people in my office and I like them all."

When she was a student nurse, Sara met Sidney Sanders. They were married for 29 years and raised two sons, Rick and Bert. Their marriage was a complete union of two people. Sara described the texture of their relationship.

"I didn't do much with other women. Aside from my work, I really did not have a separate life. All we wanted was to be with each other. Sidney planned all our weekends together, biking for five hours, going out with friends, attending concerts and theater, having dinner parties. He would call me at work ten times a day! I just wanted to be with Sid. Perhaps I was too emotionally dependent on him, but today I have no regrets for all the time we spent together."

Sara spoke of her years with Sid with great joy. "I was absolutely content with my life. If someone had asked me on a scale of 1-15 how happy I was, I would have said '20.' Was there anything I would change? Absolutely not. I loved my life, my home, and my children. I was a very happy, contented person. I was never excited about *things*. There was nothing I wanted.

"We loved a walk in the woods, a play, traveling to new places. Sid and I played together. He planned constantly. Do and run, do and run—that was Sidney. Occasionally I would be tired and suggest that we stay home. He would say, 'Staying home is for old people. When we're old, we'll stay home.'"

At age 44, Sid had bypass surgery. He recovered well and for fifteen years he did well, leading a normal, active life. Then in January of 1993, he developed fluid on his lungs. A doctor in the outpatient clinic of the hospital removed the fluid. When Sara and Sid told the doctor of their plans to attend the theater in Chicago that weekend, he assured them they could go.

On Friday evening, Sara prepared a lovely dinner using her best silver and china. Later on that night Sidney felt ill, and Sara took him to the emergency room. The diagnosis was lung congestion, and he was given antibiotics for what seemed to be a minor ailment, easily treatable. When their son Bert arrived at the hospital, the situation seemed well in hand.

"Dad's fine," Sara told Bert. "You can go home."

Suddenly Sid hyperventilated. Sara called a nurse, who arrived and shooed her out of the room, but not before Sara saw Sidney's eyes roll back.

"I am a nurse. I knew what I was seeing. I knew that he had died. I was absolutely hysterical. I was screaming and screaming. All I remember was that someone called the hospital chaplain."

All efforts to revive Sidney failed. In a split second her adored husband was gone.

Sidney's sudden death was a seismic shock that reverberated for days and months in thunderous waves of disbelief and denial for Sara. Adjusting to the upheaval in her life was long and arduous for Sara. "When Sid died, for the first two weeks I was practically non-functional. Then for several months I experienced unpredictable, erratic mood changes from day to day. I'd feel good, and then I would feel incredibly sad for months.

"Every day I got up. I went to work, I came home, I went to bed. My work saved me. It was the only part of my life that remained exactly the same. Everything else in my life had to be restructured, remolded. I was so grateful for a place to go where I could function normally. I returned to a very supportive environment. Work was my structure and my salvation."

In the early weeks and months, Sara was so preoccupied that she frequently lost things: her credit card, her house keys, and her car keys. At work she filled the coffee maker with water, added the coffee and forgot to place the pot underneath. Coffee spewed all over the room. "At times I thought I was losing my mind," she confessed. "Fortunately this phase ended soon and without dire results."

Sid had been a successful attorney, a sole practitioner. He also was involved in rehabbing, owning, and managing several properties of his own. Although Sara had visited the office often, she was not at all familiar with its organization or contents. Within weeks of Sid's death, Sara began the process of liquidating the business, closing the office, and going through files and records. Overwhelmed and distraught as she was, Sara knew that she and she alone must do the work.

"I still don't know how I got through that. It took two months. Now it was all my responsibility and it was important to me to do a good job.

When Sara's own workday was over, she collected herself, shifted gears, and went to her "other" job. After closing down the office, she brought home all the business records of the past five years. Often Sara watched her tears rolling across legal documents, as she touched all the papers that so recently were in Sid's hands. Evaluating and disposing of 25 boxes of client records was daunting.

Somewhere in all the turmoil, Sara lost her self-confidence and self-esteem. Suddenly this confident, self-assured woman was plagued with insecurity in every aspect of her life.

"I felt unsure being alone. I was insecure in financial matters, in my job, in social situations. I felt devalued as a person. I really don't quite understand my insecurity because I had been very independent. I had my own career that I loved. I guess I didn't realize how much of my self-image was tied up in Sid and in our couplehood. When Sid died, I was devastated. Regaining my self-esteem took a long time.

"My emotions were like a roller coaster. Every emotion was heightened. I couldn't even listen to the radio because sounds were exaggerated in my ears. I could only be with one or two people at a time, not with a group. I couldn't listen to trite conversation. And of course, I had no time or energy or emotional strength to 'make plans.' If a friend called me, fine. I would go out. For two years I could not call friends to initiate plans."

Physical problems appeared too. For the first time in her life, Sara began to have headaches. Worst of all, she couldn't sleep because she had so much on her mind. Chamomile tea was the only remedy that seemed to help. After the long days she was putting in, she would go to bed, toss and turn, then would doze off for an hour or two, then switch on the TV, and sleep again for a short while. For months, she was exhausted.

Sara said, "Of course, my sons were my greatest support. They were patient with me, they were so concerned, and we spent a lot of time together. I could never have gone through those early months without their loving care, their hugs, their visits, and their phone calls."

It was Sid's other interest, real estate, that gave Sara the focus which enabled her to move forward. Several months after Sid's death she decided to maintain the properties and manage them for at least two years. "It would not have been intelligent to make any major changes right away. Many people told me that and I knew they were right."

Because Sara had assisted Sid with the property management business, she had the knowledge base and skills to continue on her own. As she talked about it, her voice reflected excitement and satisfaction. "I amazed myself. I worked full-time and did real estate management for four years alone. I handled all the day-to-day work—coordinating repairs, showing apartments, hiring painters, purchasing carpet. Between my job and the real estate, I worked seven days a week, 15 or 16 hours a day. I was lucky if I had an hour a day to myself."

Many times Sara considered selling the real estate business. "Finally the work was just too much for me so I consulted with two property managers. Should I sell?"

The consultants advised Sara that these were very good properties, and that it was in her best interest to hire a property manager. That is exactly what she did. The decision was a good one, emotionally and financially. Having a property manager relieved Sara of the daily, time-consuming demands, allowing her time for herself. Maintaining the business in this more efficient way provided Sara with a different challenge and a new sense of pride in her accomplishment.

The other source of renewal for Sara began not long after Sid died. Always a physically active person, Sara began to run to relieve her stress. As the days went by, she was soon running a mile or two. The running felt good. Gradually Sara began running three or four times a week. The more she ran, the more she enjoyed it.

"I was under so much pressure, for a very long time—probably three years—trying to untangle my life, working full time, and managing properties. Running was a good stress reliever. Gradually I began to run six or seven days a week because it helped me so much. It has been an integral part of my healing.

"Today running gives me a tremendous amount of energy to do all the things I still do, morning to night. It makes me feel good about myself, about my physical well-being. It helps me in my work, in my mental capacity. I do my best thinking when I run. My goal is someday to run a marathon."

Taking a deep breath, Sara smiled, "Now I enjoy everything again. I am very grateful for my life. I have season tickets to six or seven series in theater and music. Today my life is full and satisfying, but I am still working on it. I fill my time with people and activities that bring pleasure and satisfaction. The journey has not been easy. When I look back over the last six years, it boggles my mind how I have evolved. One important thing I have realized is that I am so much more capable than I thought."

I don't recall what Sara wore that cold February day. I only know that she brought me what I needed at that moment, hope. One moment we were strangers; the next, she held my soul in her palm. No veil of social grace separated us. When her hands touched mine, they brought gentle support and serene understanding.

When my tears came, she wrapped her slim arms around me and let me cry. I looked up and saw her clouded blue eyes blink back her own tears, tears for me, tears for herself, tears for every wife who has shared our loss. In that moment Sara became my mother, my stepmother, and my aunts who were gone and could not be there to hold me.

That day Sara and I sat together on the soft chenille sofa for two hours—or a few minutes—sharing apricots and the tender compassion of two women who knew grief, one who had learned to survive, and one who would.

ଔ   ଔ   ଔ

SARA'S APRICOT CHICKEN

Combine one jar apricot preserves with one package dry onion soup mix.
Heat over low heat until it all melts together.
Add some finely chopped garlic.
Pour mixture over chicken pieces.
Bake at 375 degrees for 45 minutes.

Add dried apricots and a sprinkling of pine nuts.
Bake another 15 minutes.

Yum!

CHAPTER 3

Twenty-One Days

In the first three weeks after Dick died, I experienced a range of emotions that confused and exhausted me. Each night I went to bed weary, awoke too early every morning, and was tired all day. Grief became a way of life for me, unpredictable in timing, but inevitable in its arrival. I learned that the triggers for grief were as numerous and varied as the triggers for joy. I wondered if I would ever be happy again.

Evenings were the most difficult time of the day. I dreaded dinnertime. Often at dinner, as I sat picking at a salad or can of tuna fish, a bout of prolonged wailing would come over me. Even as I wept, I knew there had to be a bottom to this wellspring of tears—I could only cry for so long. After three or five or ten minutes, my tears subsided.

Because I could not bear to watch TV yet, in the evening I would call a friend or read a little, hoping to doze off. During the night I often awoke from a light sleep to find my face wet from tears I didn't remember shedding.

At times, I wept quietly, overcome with feelings of sadness for my vital, vigorous husband, cut down at 61. I ached at the realization that Dick would never see another football game, eat another caramel cashew custard, hear another Mozart symphony, or hold a first grandchild. This had been a happy second marriage for both of us, less than twelve years old. Our dreams for a long future together had ended in a moment. I cried for the loss of our comfortable *we* and *us*. No day passed without tears of regret for all those losses.

Just looking in my pantry broke me up. On the shelf were the foods Dick loved, particularly the popcorn and flavorings and the four bottles of Tabasco sauce. When I finally opened Dick's closet and saw the neat rows of sport coats matched with slacks, the business suits so carefully hung, the polished shoes waiting for a walk, I sat on the floor and cried.

Occasionally, I sobbed in apprehension of the responsibilities I would now face alone. I knew that these were really tears of self-pity, but my wound was too fresh to start planning my future.

I never knew what might provoke my tears—a word, a memory, a thought. My outbursts felt like trains that approached from the distance, gradually accelerated as they barreled toward me, and then ramrodded me with full force. There was no stopping them. Several times I had meltdowns while I was driving the car.

In public I choked back the grief that came when I saw couples together, holding hands or exchanging a glance.

I would feel rocky when I saw an acquaintance for the first time, someone who hadn't been at the funeral. She would offer sympathy and a hug, and my tears would begin as though I were experiencing the shock all over again.

One day my grief was reflected in the eyes and the words of a friend that I met in the grocery store. A look of shock crossed her face. In a quiet voice, she asked, "How are you doing?" Doing? I bristled a little at the question. I had no idea how I was doing. I wanted to ask, "Compared to what? How do I gauge how I'm doing? Is there a grade on grieving?"

When Sara had asked me the same question, it was with a heart that would understand the full answer. Then I realized that the woman in the store was simply being kind. This was her way of letting me know that she was aware of my loss and wanted to express concern. I answered, "Thanks, I'm doing okay. One day at a time, you know." But, of course, she didn't know.

In early February, my good friends Lisa and Jeff invited me to join them for dinner the following Sunday night. My first instinct was that I was not ready to go out to a restaurant. When I hesitated, Lisa encouraged me. She and Jeff really wanted to see me. We would go to a quiet place nearby. I accepted the invitation. As the week went by, I actually began to look forward to going out. Perhaps it would be good for me.

On Sunday night, I selected my favorite brown wool slacks and matching sweater, and carefully added my nicest leather belt, bright jewelry and a colorful scarf. It was the first time I had bothered to put on make-up or worry about my hair, and that too felt good, life-enhancing.

When Lisa and Jeff arrived to pick me up, I slid into the back seat of the car. Suddenly, I felt a dull ache. As I looked over at the wide, empty expanse beside me and saw my friends sitting together in front, I had a moment of piercing sadness, remembering how only a short time ago, I had been a wife in the front seat, half of a couple. I tried to look out the window and push aside my pain.

Arriving at the restaurant, we were ushered to a table for four. I sat between my two friends, opposite an empty chair. Soon the waitress came, glanced around the table, looked directly at me, and asked, "Will there be a fourth person joining you?" I couldn't speak. Lisa answered for me, and the waitress took away the place setting. Completely unaware, the waitress smiled at us and announced the specials for the evening. My dear friends looked at me with compassion, smiled softly, and asked what I might enjoy for dinner.

After placing our orders, Lisa and Jeff began to chat about the latest snowstorm and what was going on in their lives. With great sensitivity, they didn't ask about my life. What pleasantries or amusing anecdotes could I possibly offer?

Through three courses, my hosts did not mention Dick's name, and neither did I. Why couldn't we talk about him? Were my friends afraid I would become upset? For my part, I felt that if we talked about Dick, in a way he would be here with us. On the other hand, I was afraid I would break down and make us all uncomfortable.

I heard about their jobs, their son's new house, and their grandchild's week at camp. My attention faded in and out as I picked at my whitefish and tried to avoid looking across the table at the empty chair. I needed to be gracious and pay attention to the conversation. They were trying so hard to lift my spirits with happy talk.

As dinner ended, they asked if I would like to go back to their house for dessert? God, no. I mumbled, "No, thank you. It was so good to be with you. Dinner was delicious, but I am really full—and very tired. Thank you so much for a lovely evening." We drove back to my house, and Lisa and Jeff watched as I stumbled to the front door. They waited until I was safely inside and drove away.

All through the evening, I knew that a juggernaut of grief was coming. Had my instincts been right? Had I gone out before I was ready? Or would this have happened no matter how long I had waited?

No sooner had I taken off my coat and gloves, than I fell into a chair and cried—huge, heaving sobs. After a few minutes, I calmed down. I went into the bathroom and glanced into the mirror. Was this the same woman who had stood there two hours before, looking composed and attractive? I looked worn and old. The make-up I had so carefully applied was wet and runny. My brown clothes seemed drab. My skin was blotchy, my eyes small and red, and the smile lines around my mouth formed a sad parenthesis around my down-turned mouth. I had never seen a face so forlorn.

I changed into my pajamas and crawled into bed. Struggling to keep my eyes open, I read one page in a book on grief, and then turned off the light. All I wanted was to escape into sleep and forget my life for a few hours. I prayed, "Thank you, God, for getting me through another really hard day. And please, ease this unbearable pain." My eyes closed and I was asleep instantly.

Tomorrow would be the twenty-second day.

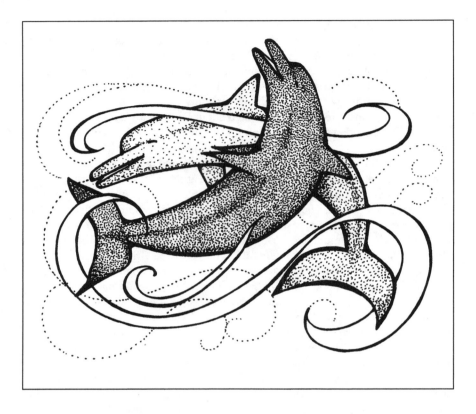

CHAPTER 4

Visitors and Voices

In those early days, Paulette and I spoke often on the phone. She was my link to Dick. I would ask her what she saw or sensed and at times she described images and conveyed words. Speaking with Paulette comforted me, whether or not she had a message. On February 3, she suggested that I try to communicate directly with Dick. That had never occurred to me. I was skeptical.

That night I fell asleep with Paulette's idea fresh in my mind. I awoke long before dawn. Aching for a sign from Dick, I pleaded, "Please, just tell me something. I need to hear from you." I waited.

Almost asleep again, I heard the words, "Please take care of Jennifer. She needs extra love and attention now."

I was so happy to hear from him that I began to cry. "I will, Dick." He was thinking of the cat, his dear little Jennifer whom he had loved. It certainly wasn't the kind of message I had sought, but it was pure Dick. All day I was more aware of Jennifer. I was sure that she missed Dick too. When she curled silently into my lap, I slowly brushed and stroked her. Soothing the cat was also soothing for me.

Hopeful because of Dick's visit, the next night I called out again, "Dick, tell me what to do, how to go on."

Silence. "See more beauty."

More silence. "Knowing is not knowing."

A long pause. Then, "There is no *time*." I tried to interpret the phrases. Did Dick want me to see more beauty in the world? Do we think we know, but what we know is nothing? Does time, as we know it, have no meaning in eternity?

Four nights passed with no messages. On February 8, in the middle of the night and in a half-awake, half-asleep state, Dick was with me again. We talked about our lives for nearly two hours, but in the morning I could only remember two phrases that I had heard: "You have the sweetest soul" and "I put up fences and defenses."

31

Going through some papers the next day, I found a copy of a letter Dick had written to an old friend and colleague, with whom he had lost touch for many years. The letter was dated a few days before we left for Hawaii. My tears fell on the pages as I read Dick's words, telling his friend about the last twelve years of our lives. Toward the end he had written, "Diane is a marvel. . . . It is a good marriage."

The same day, in the back of a desk drawer, I found a beautiful letter from my dad to Dick on his 50th birthday. Dad had written, "What I wish you today is that you can make every day a happy and healthy one so you can enjoy the next 27 years as much as I have. In retrospect, I find I have completely forgotten all the unpleasant things and only remember the happy times. I don't know whether God, in His infinite wisdom, planned it that way, or if it's just the nature of the beast in me. You will make the same statement in the year 2015. (I have some bonds coming due in 2015, so hang around.)"

I read and reread both the letters and cried for two men who had loved life and whom I had loved. Finding those letters was a special gift.

The rest of the day was grueling. Hours of bookkeeping, updating records in the computer, and paying bills exhausted me, but I pushed myself to complete the work because I knew Dick would want me to. I cried off and on all day; I could feel the pressure building up inside me.

A few days before, my friend Nancy had suggested a session with a special kind of therapist who she thought could relieve some of my stress and anxiety. Grateful for her concern and willing to try anything that might help, I agreed to go. The appointment was that evening. Nancy hand-delivered me to the office. I had no idea what lay ahead. Nancy had been unable to describe the process, and I was too weary to question. In the office, I picked up a card: "Chuck Eigen: Rolfing, Craniosacrial, Focusing, Body-Mind Therapies." I still had no idea what to expect.

From my first moment with Chuck, I felt completely at ease. From his soft voice and his compassionate eyes, I knew that he was a person who would understand my grief and would be open to hearing about my mystical experiences—and I needed to talk about them. I closed my eyes. Aware of my loss, he asked if I wanted to speak about it. As I spoke, Chuck listened silently while lightly touching my neck, head, shoulders, spine, and back. When I finished, he said this was a beautiful story, and that I had received a great gift in Paulette. He sensed great "synchronicity" in all that had happened. After I had recited the "conversations" I had had with Dick and my dad, I sighed and said, "They are as good as anything we know."

"Better," he said emphatically.

Chuck said that I had opened up my own soul and that I should continue the dialogues with Dick. "Relationships never end. Dick is very present with you now."

He explained to me that grieving is organic and that it takes its own course. "You keep reliving the shock and asking, 'Why did it happen? How did it happen?

Did it really happen?'" Chuck was right. These were exactly the questions that echoed through my brain several times a day. He explained that this is the mind trying to process and integrate what has happened.

He suggested that I not try to subdue my feelings but rather that I put boundaries on my grief by taking an hour or two each day to read, to cry, to meditate—whatever I needed to do. He urged me to do some intensive journaling, writing down my experiences and emotions. I told him that I had begun writing a diary even before the funeral so that I would remember all the events and conversations. He was certain that writing would be therapeutic for me. Strangely, I had not thought of that, but I realized it was true.

I left Chuck's office feeling more relaxed than I had been in two weeks. A day that had begun in tension had ended with my receiving a special gift. In the evening I took a long bath in the mineral salts Nancy had given me. My blood pressure was way down. I could hardly believe how tranquil I felt.

At 3:15 in the morning, I awoke to Dick's words. "I'll be with you as you let me be with you . . . Tomorrow I'll be with you a lot. You will have a good day."

"Why did you go?" I asked plaintively.

"It had to be."

"Are you happy?"

"Oh, yes—better than happy." Pause. Then: "I will send you people who will help you. I will be present. No fences and defenses. Sweetie, stop anguishing."

"Do you know how much I love you?" I asked.

"I know, Sweetie."

I fell back into a deep sleep and awoke to a bright, sunny day. I felt more like my old self. That night I received another message from Dick: "Accept all love. (Pause) It was time. (Pause) You're doing well with the business stuff. (Pause) Please call my clients."

A few nights passed with no visits. On February 11, I heard Dick's voice again, another riddle: "It's all temporal." All of what? All of life? *Temporal*— fleeting or insignificant?

The next night we had a dialogue. I said, "I miss you so much."

"I know. . . . You will be whole. You will have peace. Try for peace."

I asked, "Do you miss me?"

"Sweetie, I'm with you. You're not with me, so it's easier for me because I'm with you and looking after you." Pause. Then he continued, "You are resourceful and strong. Remember, there is no *time*. You will be whole. You will have peace. You're doing right to call upon people to help you. You have many friends who love you and care about you. Call upon them."

I asked again, "Are you happy?"

"More than happy."

I had another question. "Would you do anything different?"

He answered, "The last eleven years I would do the same. Before that, you could say I did it my way. There are many here who did it their way. They just come here a little sooner."

I began to cry. "I just miss you so much."

"I know, Sweetie. Cry all you need to. Nourish and nurture yourself." Then he repeated, "You will be whole. You will have peace."

In that moment, I thought about our friend Howard, his spiritual approach to life, and the story of the dolphins.

I asked. "What about Howard?"

The answer came instantly, "He is closer than the rest of us. I wasn't there yet."

On Friday night, Margie and I went to Shabbat services at our synagogue where Dick had always been so happy and peaceful. During the service the cantor chanted the beautiful, "*Mishebeyrach*," a prayer for the recovery of loved ones who are ill. Tears rolled down my face. My loved one would not recover.

When the congregation stood to recite the *Kaddish*, the prayer for remembering the dead, every syllable hammered at my heart: You're gone, you're gone. The last time, you were here reading *Kaddish* with me. Now I'm reading *Kaddish* for you. *How can that be?* After the service, the congregation gathered to sing the blessings over the bread and the wine. In my memory, I saw Dick and me standing there together, only a few weeks ago, as we too sang with joy. I began to cry. Several friends put their arms around me and held me until this wave of grief passed.

When we returned home, Margie asked where the Scrabble board was. I could hardly remember. It had been at least five years since we had played. We found the set and spent the next two hours moving around the tiles and concocting words. We even laughed at some of our efforts. To my surprise the game absorbed and calmed me. What a stroke of genius on the part of my sensitive and loving daughter.

In the middle of the night, I experienced what I have heard described as panic attacks: tightness in my head, palpable anxiety, sweats. Just before dawn, I had another visitor. "Diane, this is Daddy."

Was I stunned? After all that had occurred in my life, I was beyond being shocked, and I was happy for my dad's visit. I needed him.

"We're all worried about you. You've got to slow down. I want you to take Shabbat tomorrow: no bookkeeping, no checkbooks, and no computer. You're just like me, feeling that you've got to do it all right now. You need to take time for you. I wish I had taken more time for me. It won't matter whether you do this work tomorrow or Monday or next week. Read, listen to music, do yoga, exercise—but no work. God was right to create Shabbat. I wish I had observed it."

I said I would try to ease up. Then I asked, "How is Mom?"

"She worries about you."

"Where is Dick?"

"He's busy, always busy. Everyone likes him. Mom loves him. Let Margie help you. She's a wonderful young woman. Diane, we all want you to stop pushing so hard and take care of yourself. And remember what Dick said, 'See more beauty.'"

I answered, "I will, Daddy. I will take Shabbat tomorrow."

And then my dad said, "Grief is so hard on people. If only you could know about here, there wouldn't be such grief—but God has His reasons that we don't know, and so there is terrible grief."

I observed Shabbat. In the morning Julie, the diver from Washington, called to see how I was. On January 25, she had returned to the beach and taken a picture, which she would send me, along with a brief article in the *Maui News* about Dick's death. I was pleased to hear from her.

A friend who had lost her son came over for lunch. When I spoke of my unusual experiences, she took it all in with easy and calm acceptance. She told me that she often talks to her son. Although I never thought I was crazy, my friend's experience was reassuring.

That afternoon, in a sudden spurt of energy, I walked on the treadmill and did a light workout. In the evening, I read, played music, ate dinner alone, and allowed myself to write five Thank You notes to people who had brought food and flowers or who had helped in other ways. I was pleased with my day. Shabbat had gone well.

Then I picked up the album of our trip to the Grand Canyon. Looking at pictures of that happy time made me mourn again for all that Dick and I had lost. Even as I deliberately pulled out more albums and turned more pages, I wondered why I was torturing myself like this. I wailed aloud, over and over, *"How can this BE? How can this BE, that you are gone?"* Finally, I closed the albums and went to bed.

At dawn I had a brief visit from my mother. She seemed more remote than my other visitors, perhaps because she had been gone so long, nearly thirty-five years. She said that she had always watched me and that she was proud of me. She said, "Feeling is healing." I wanted to shout, When, Mom, when? When will all this pain be healing?

A week later, I had a new and unexpected visitor, Frances, my stepmother, who had died the past July and whom I had loved dearly. Just as in life, she was supportive. In a clear voice, she said, "You will have a good and joyful life."

A few nights later, after many days' absence, Dick was there. He said only three sentences, "You are not alone. I am holding you. Remember, you are not alone."

For our last Chanukah, Dick had given me a long-stemmed rose dipped in gold. "This is for my Sweetie," he had said, proudly. Usually at Chanukah, we would purchase something practical for the house. I was touched that he had been inspired to make such a romantic gesture.

When I woke up on Valentine's Day, I picked up the rose, which was lying on a velvet scarf on my dresser. I ran my hands over the smooth surface. It was as though he had known he wouldn't be here, so he had given me my Valentine's gift early, a very special gift—bright, solid, and lasting. I cried for a few minutes and placed the rose back on the cloth. Many times that day I walked by the rose and held it. My first Valentine's Day alone didn't seem quite so lonely.

March 1 marked the end of *Sheloshim,* the thirty days set aside in Judaism for intensive mourning. At the beginning I had thought, "If I can just make it through the first thirty days." Then the milestone was two months. Simply surviving became the goal. One day blurred into the next. I missed having no one to tell "Good morning" and "Good night," greetings that delineate one day from the next. I groped my way through the long days. I brought food into the house, listened to music, and attended the Grief Group at the synagogue. When I left my own doorstep, I felt like a spectator, watching people who were part of a world I had left. Sometimes I asked myself the question I heard so often from others, "How are you doing?" My truthful answer was, "Some days are better than others."

By mid-March, my life fell into a new pattern. I could take an interest in other people's lives or laugh at something amusing, but tears were never far away. One weekend I had to go into the mall to do an errand. I saw couples laughing and chatting, and I had a flashback of all the times Dick and I had shopped here together. I forgot my errand, raced out of the mall, and rushed home.

I had not yet learned to fill my weekends to the brim. When Dick was alive, it didn't matter whether we had plans or not—we had each other for company. One Saturday in March, I faced a full day and evening by myself because I had not made any plans. By afternoon, I was desperate to see another human being. I decided to call Marlene, a friend who had not been able to visit because of her work schedule. When I heard her voice, I began to sob. It was hard to say the words, but I told her that I was having a really hard day and that I needed her. She came over right away. I was so grateful that I clung to her. She couldn't stay long, but even that hour shortened the day and sustained me for a few hours. I didn't feel quite so isolated from the world. She thanked *me* for calling her!

For six weeks, I had been determined not to indulge in self-pity. I had tried to be strong, not allowing myself that particular emotion. But on that Saturday, I felt sorry for myself. I had lost the focus of my life; I had lost my moorings. Wasn't I entitled to a little self-pity? That night I gave myself permission to wallow a little, and those tears were a kind of a release.

Between three and four in the morning, I woke up. I cried out to Dick, "I miss you so much. I need you *here*, with me!"

The answer was slow and sure. "All else is possible."

"Then I want to dream about you."

I dozed off again, and later Dick appeared in a dream. He had come back home, as though returning from a trip. He was unaware that anything unusual had happened to us. In my sleep, I was very happy.

Every night I looked forward to the possibility of more visits. What did I believe about the visitors and voices? Had I been talking to myself, or had the words I heard come from somewhere else? I didn't look for rational answers. It was enough that I had a source of great solace.

As the days and weeks passed, and I began to take more steps back into normal life, the nocturnal visits were fewer and farther between. It felt as though the window to that other world was slowly closing. Perhaps my need had diminished; maybe I was moving forward.

I was glad to see the sun every morning, to know that one more day separated me from January 24. Sometimes I clutched at the words, "Remember, you are not alone. I am holding you." Sometimes I just thought about the dolphins.

CHAPTER 5

Adam's Chair

On a chilly Tuesday morning in mid-February, I attended my first meeting of the Grief Group at our synagogue, and there I met Naomi Golden. Across the table from me sat a cheerful, smiling lady with sparkling light brown eyes. When the members introduced themselves, I learned that Naomi had lost her husband Nathan nearly five years ago.

Dark loose curls framed her soft, pretty face. At about 5'7", Naomi had the gentle curves that would invite a grandchild or two to curl up on her lap. A bouncing energy emanated from her. Here was a woman who didn't sit still very much. Her laughter was hearty and infectious. Instead of laughing after telling you something amusing, Naomi laughed first, advance notice that you would soon be joining her. She seemed a completely happy person, like someone who has never seen a dark day in her life.

When I visited Naomi, we sat down for tea and a delicious homemade coffeecake. She spoke of her life.

Naomi's parents were married in Poland in 1932, and within days her father sailed for South America. He worked his way north through several countries, finally arriving in Costa Rica. After five years he had saved enough to bring over his bride, who arrived on New Year's Day of 1938. Naomi was born in Costa Rica in 1940. Nine years later the family, which now included Naomi and her brother, immigrated to the United States, settling in the Midwest.

Naomi was fluent in Spanish and Yiddish. Although English is her third language, Naomi never had an accent. She laughed as she recalled her childish pride in sounding very American. "Now I'd love an exotic foreign accent!"

To this day, when Naomi can't quite find the word she wants, her children say, "We know, Mom. English is your third language!"

Naomi and Nathan married in 1958, when Naomi was barely 18. She had planned to go on to college, but decided to marry instead. At 19, she was a mom; by age 26, she had five children, three girls and twin boys. Naomi did what moms did in those days: she ran her home and raised her children.

Nathan owned and operated a second-generation factory that manufactured industrial boots. A born salesman with a keen sense of business and marketing, he took over the family business and it prospered. He worked hard and was proud of what he built. He loved his business and he loved his boots.

Nathan's business allowed the Goldens to enjoy doing what they loved best, entertaining, dancing, dining out, and traveling. Their favorite vacation spot was Waikiki Beach in Hawaii, where they would spend two weeks relaxing, walking on the beach, swimming, riding the waves, eating in good restaurants, and sipping a drink by the pool at sunset. For weekend getaways, they would jump on a plane for Las Vegas, where they both enjoyed the people and the shows.

"I have marvelous memories," she smiled. "Nathan lived the old adage, 'Work hard, play hard.' He always said, 'Live for today.' And we did. We had fun together."

This long, wonderful marriage lasted until April 2, 1994, when Nathan died of esophageal cancer, a devastating illness that he fought valiantly until the end. He was a gregarious man who loved to schmooze and had to try every new restaurant in town. When Nathan lost his ability to speak and to eat, his daily losses isolated him from friends and activities he loved. As his world compressed to his home, then to his room, then to his bed, Naomi became his entire life, encouraging him every day with her loving smile and upbeat personality.

As though she wanted a respite from reliving her sadness, Naomi stood up, smiled at me, and asked, "How would you like a grand tour of our family?" And she led me to a wall teeming with family pictures. It was easy to follow the chronology, to peek in on weddings, bar mitzvahs, birthday parties, growing children and grandchildren, and Naomi and Nathan smiling among their progeny. Naomi told me everyone's names with pride and anecdotes. My eyes stopped on a picture of a beautiful little boy with grey-blue eyes, curly brown hair, and a dash of freckles. He was curled up on his grandfather's lap.

"Who is that?" I asked.

"This is Adam, our youngest grandchild," said Naomi. "He adored Nathan, called him Grampy." Naomi sighed. "That picture was taken about a year before Nathan died. Maybe because Adam was so young, he was never even aware of how thin and frail his grandfather was becoming. When Adam came over, he would go right to Nathan, climb up on his lap, and later onto his bed, and play with him. He even visited him in the hospital. Adam was so attached to his Grampy." Naomi's eyes filled and so did mine.

After Nathan died, Naomi felt a terrible loss, loss of her lifelong friend and the happy life they shared. "For many months after Nathan died, I woke up and cried aloud and alone in my house. It was a kind of relief. Sometimes it feels good to cry."

"How did you go on?" I asked.

Naomi took a deep breath. She told me that she has always had a sunny disposition. Her life with Nathan was so untroubled, so apple-pie normal. Would Nathan's death change her?

"When all of this happened to me, I was determined that, no matter what, I would not become a bitter, selfish woman who felt sorry for herself. Do you know that Yiddish word *farbissene*? It's just what it sounds like. You see people who are bitter and angry. I never wanted to be that way. The rabbi helped me with that. I don't know how I would have handled this if not for my involvement with the Tuesday morning group. It has helped me so much."

In 1994, a new widow requested that the synagogue offer a Grief Group, particularly for younger widows, women in their 50s. Rabbi Barry Silberg responded immediately, and the support group had been meeting most Tuesday mornings at 11 A.M. for the past five years. Naomi was a charter member.

"Every week I come away with new insights. The rabbi is a wonderful teacher. Let me give you an example. A few months after Nathan died, I was invited to a wedding out of town. How could I handle it? It was too soon. I dreaded it, but I had no real excuse. Do I go or not go? I didn't know what to do."

When Naomi described her dilemma, the rabbi asked her two questions, "Will you know anyone else at the wedding? Will there be some friends or family you would like to be with?"

"I don't know anyone else who's going," she answered.

"Why would you put yourself into that situation?" asked the rabbi. "What would you have to gain? Why go somewhere that you have absolutely no support?"

Naomi did not go to the wedding. "It was wonderful to have that answer and that realistic perspective from the rabbi. Most people would have said, 'Oh, go ahead. You'll have fun.' Not going was the right decision. Then and there I learned that I don't have to subject myself to situations that will cause me pain."

Naomi spoke more about the first year.

"I wouldn't have done half as well if I hadn't met the women in the support group. We have talked, cried with each other, called each other on our *yahrzeits*, the anniversaries of our husbands' deaths. I can't tell you how many times I sit in awe of these women and think how fortunate I am to have met them. They are my lifeline. It is sad that it took Nathan's death to know these women."

She continued, "Of course, I have my children, and they are wonderful—all our children are wonderful—but it's different. They look upon us differently." To our children, as well as to the outside world, we were now in a new category, we had an altered status. Naomi simply accepted this fact.

"The kids miss their dad, but their daily lives haven't been turned upside down like mine. The women—they are the ones who truly understand."

Naomi's tone changed as she told me what happened after Nathan died.

"I had some terrible situations," Naomi said. I tensed, wondering what more could possibly have happened to this dear woman. A line from Shakespeare flashed through my mind: "When troubles come, they come not in single spies but in battalions."

Naomi explained, "Another kind of death occurred a year after Nathan died when my daughter went through a difficult divorce. I couldn't sit and feel sorry for myself. I had to be there for her."

Then Naomi told me about her mom. "Two years later, in 1997, my mother, who was my rock of Gibraltar, had a heart attack and needed angioplasty. She came through the surgery very well, but she refused to eat the hospital food because it was during Passover, and she refused to touch any food that was not especially prepared—Kosher for Passover.

"The next morning I arrived at the hospital with a box of matzos for her. The doctor saw me, called me aside, and told me that my mother had taken a turn for the worse and that she was dying," Naomi's voice quavered a little. "That whole day my children, my brother, and I sat with her and held her hand to let her know that we were all there. All that day, over and over, we sang to her *My Yiddishe Mama*. It was hard. All this happened within three years. That was a lot."

Without missing a beat, she continued, "I can't stand people who ask, 'Why me?' I don't want to listen. Through all of Nathan's suffering, he never once asked, 'Why me?'"

As Naomi told me her story, I saw her growing stronger. From so much heartache had emerged a confident, independent woman, who never lost her gentle ways. "I had never realized the strength I have within. When I married, my husband made most of the decisions. It worked for us and probably for most of my generation.

"In 35 years, the only trip I ever planned was to Israel—and that was because I was the one who wanted to go. 'You want to go, you plan it!' Nathan said, and I did. We took all the children, who were teenagers at the time, and my mother. The trip was not only educational but highly emotional as well because we met family members whom we had never met before. It was a very special experience for all of us. Until the day she died, my mother glowed when she recalled our wonderful trip to Israel." Naomi paused, then added, "I think planning that trip helped prepare me for my life now."

I asked, "Do you feel good making decisions for yourself?"

"I do feel good that I am able to make decisions on my own," she replied. "It has been hard, especially in business matters, but when I work through the challenge, I feel that I'm growing." Naomi chuckled, "Actually, I'm pretty good at it!"

As naturally as people are drawn to Naomi, so is she drawn to others. "I love being with people. I don't care where I go as long as I'm with people. If someone says, 'Let's go to dinner. Where do you want to go?' I'll answer, 'I don't care. You decide.'" Then she laughed, "But that doesn't mean I won't complain about the food!"

When I asked Naomi what else sustains her, she answered, "I try to keep myself busy. The pain of being alone comes and goes. But sometimes it feels like I take a step forward and two backward. I guess that too is part of the process. When I'm busy, that's when I'm at my best."

Based on my limited experience, I volunteered, "I guess planning is the key thing."

Emphatically, Naomi declared, "It's more than that. It's a full-time job!" Naomi learned to keep her calendar full, particularly on the hard days—holidays and weekends. Early on she made sure that she had plans to go out to dinner or to a movie with friends. Eventually she planned vacations with friends and family. She volunteered to babysit for her grandchildren. Naomi created a full and busy life.

Our conversation returned to the Grief Group. "You know, after five years, people ask me why I keep going. I tell them that I'm glad to be here for new people. When you're going through it, you wonder, 'Is this the way I'm supposed to feel?' I can tell them that what they're feeling and doing is normal. It also helps me in ways I wouldn't have foreseen."

When one woman lost a younger sister, she described her conflicted feelings. "After my sister died, I put my sadness for my husband on a back burner. I felt guilty about that, like I had deserted him. But I know I love him just as much."

Naomi sighed, "That was what happened to me when I lost my mother. I felt guilty that I was neglecting Nathan. In listening to my friend, I realized I needn't feel that way. Grieving a new loss did not change my friend's love for her husband nor my love for Nathan. I could just hold so much sorrow at a time. It helped to know this. My guilt left me."

Her voice perked up. "Would you like to see a great picture of Nathan? Come to the den with me. I have something to show you."

We went downstairs and entered a paneled room with a desk, toys, an old high chair, and a treadmill. When I asked how long she had been exercising, she answered. "Now that is another story. Would you like to hear it?"

I nodded.

"Sometimes at Valentine's Day, I would drop clues to Nathan about what I would like. When I opened the gift that I had hinted at, I would act completely surprised.

"That first Valentine's Day was tough. I dreaded it. One morning in early February I saw a full-page ad for treadmills. I love to walk but the weather was too cold to go outside, and I needed to keep exercising. So I made a decision. I marched out the door and drove straight over to the fitness equipment store."

On Valentine's Day, the doorbell rang. Two burly men announced a delivery for Mrs. Golden. Naomi escorted the men to the den, where they unpacked the crate and set up the treadmill. Attached to the box was a large card that read, "Use me in good health! From Naomi to Naomi with love."

"I turned on the machine, climbed on, and said aloud, 'Why, thank you so much! That's exactly what I wanted! What a surprise!'"

We both laughed.

"Now," said Naomi, leading me across the room, "Here is Nathan." She pointed to a huge poster, an enlarged photograph of Nathan Golden standing in his factory. He was smiling broadly, surrounded by huge bins overflowing with boots.

Naomi explained that the picture was part of a citywide exhibit on small businesses. When the exhibit closed, the poster came home. Nathan wanted to hang it in the bedroom, but Naomi put her foot down. "One Nathan in here is enough!"

She urged him to take the poster to the factory, but he hung it in the den. It never came down.

"I'm down here nearly every day because the walking makes me feel good," said Naomi. "And nearly every day I talk to Nathan. Sometimes I get angry with him for leaving me. Then I just say, 'I miss you terribly, but I am carrying on.'"

At first it was hard for Naomi to look at the poster. Her last image of Nathan was not the fun-loving, articulate man she married, but a sick, weary, debilitated man. She could hardly remember the strong, hearty man on the poster.

One Tuesday, the Grief Group talked about healing. A woman asked, "How do you know when you are healing?"

The rabbi quietly answered the question, "You will know you're healing when in your memories and in your mind you see your husband strong and healthy."

"And he was right," said Naomi. "It took many months and many miles on the treadmill, but today that is how I see him. Nathan is the man in the poster."

Everyone says that it is the *firsts* of the first year that are the most difficult, and the Jewish holidays can be distressing. We think, "Last year at this time, he was here."

Our holidays are spiritual times, times when our families gather together. At Rosh Hashanah and Yom Kippur, we attend services in a synagogue. Passover, the most universally observed holiday, is home- and family-centered. In observant families, for weeks before the holiday, the mother cleans the house, cooks vast stores of special foods, disposes of all bread products, and changes over to special Passover dishes. Complaints about the amount of work are forgotten in anticipation of the wonderful holiday.

At Passover children and grandchildren are sources of a special joy because they embody the continuity of our families, stretching ahead to new generations, linking past and future.

On the first night families and friends gather in our homes for the *Seder*, a traditional meal and service that retells the story of the Israelites' deliverance from slavery in Egypt, the long journey to freedom, the receiving of the Ten Commandments. At the head of the table sits the patriarch, who leads the service.

Nathan Golden died during Passover in 1994. A year later, for the first time in 35 years, Naomi faced the holiday without her husband. Of course the holiday meal would be at her home, as always. Everyone would be there except for one branch of the family that was unable to come because of a new baby.

One day while she was preparing the chicken soup, Naomi's eyes teared as she remembered Nathan's last *Seder*, just one year ago, when Adam, eighteen months old, left his toys in the living room, toddled over to the table, and nestled into Grampy's lap.

Over the next few weeks Naomi went through all the motions, trying to recapture the happy feelings of years past. At times she found herself caught up in the frenzy of preparations. Still, one thought gnawed in her mind. For weeks she anguished. Who would sit at the head of the table, in Nathan's chair? In her mind's eye, Naomi saw Nathan in his chair, beaming proudly at his family, pouring the wine, breaking the matzah, encouraging everyone to take part in the service. He was the pillar of strength for this growing family. Naomi couldn't bear to see the chair empty, nor could she bear to think of anyone else sitting there.

On Passover evening, the family arrived with the usual flurry of hugs and greetings. Each of Naomi's children in turn glanced at the table and saw that it was set as always. And there was Dad's chair, the blue captain's chair, where Nathan had sat every Passover. In front of it was a full place setting. No one dared to question Naomi, but each of her children looked at her with concern. When it was time to begin, the family moved slowly toward the dining room.

"Everyone sit down, please," said Naomi with her gentle authority. Then she walked around and took the hand of her little grandson, the beautiful child who had had such a special connection to his grandfather.

"Here, sweetheart," Naomi said to the child, "You come sit here in Grampy's chair, right next to me."

His small, freckled face turned upward as he looked at her with his serious eyes. With studied care and concentration, the little boy climbed up. His small body molded itself naturally into his grandfather's chair.

Sitting up very straight, Adam Jonathan Robinson looked around at his family and announced proudly, "This Adam's chair now!"

THE MAUI NEWS – Tuesday, February 2, 1999 – A3

■

Heart attack killed diver, autopsy results show

WAILEA — A visitor who was pulled from the water at Ulua Beach while scuba diving last week died of a massive heart attack, preliminary autopsy results show.

The man was identified as Richard Kaimen of Milwaukee, Wis.

Police were called to the beach in Wailea at 11:41 a.m. Jan. 24, with a caller reporting that cardiopulmonary resuscitation was being performed on the man after he was pulled from the ocean.

He was taken to Maui Memorial Medical Center, where he was pronounced dead.

CHAPTER 6

A Week of Torment

As the months passed, many elements of Dick's death disturbed me, particularly from the medical perspective. While the prognosis for a patient with six 12-year old bypasses, a heart attack (1992) and angioplasty (1994) is not necessarily encouraging, many people do live. Had Dick died before his time, medically speaking? Or, in truth, had he been on "borrowed time"? Had his last few years been a gift?

Since the previous summer, Dick had complained off and on about chest pain and tiredness. The doctor was never alarmed. On December 29, Dick dressed in his gray sweat suit for his periodic stress test at the hospital. Maybe now he would find out why he was hurting. He returned home too soon. He explained that the test was not scheduled, and the staff didn't have time to fit him in. He was to come back in May.

How had this happened? Dick was very precise about appointments. Still, anyone can make a mistake. Whatever the snafu, for months I asked myself what might have been different if Dick had taken the stress test that day. Would the test have revealed a problem that would have precluded scuba diving? Would Dick still be alive?

Two friends from Dick's cardiac rehab group told me that one day the men were discussing all the pills they were taking. Dick listened intently and then said very seriously, "You guys are a lot sicker than I am, and you'll both outlive me." Separately, each man told me of this incident. Did Dick have a premonition?

One evening, Dick's longtime friend and football buddy called to ask if he might come by to talk to me. Bob told me that on two occasions, in November and December, Dick was "popping nitro's." At a ball game in Green Bay, Dick had explained that he was so excited about the game that his heart was racing. In early January, when Dick was visiting Bob's home, he became very flushed and then pale. Obviously he was having some distress. Bob strongly urged his friend to see a doctor, especially before going diving. How painful this was for Bob to tell me and for me to hear, knowing that maybe things might have been different had Dick heeded the warnings. I tried not to dwell on these thoughts, but that was difficult.

What I really needed to hear was that nothing could have prevented Dick's death. If he had been lying in a beach chair in Hawaii or on the sofa at home, he would have died. Although nothing could change the reality, I needed greater peace. Verification that his death was inevitable was of the greatest importance to me. Maybe the autopsy would tell us what happened, other than the "massive heart attack" indicated in the preliminary report. Maybe I would have some peace at last.

By April I felt myself beginning to function with greater awareness of people and activities around me. When I left the security of my house, I felt less like an alien. I went out to lunch and enjoyed my friends' company and a good salad or a gooey dessert. I saw one or two movies and actually became absorbed in the plots, a respite from my own life. I still cried but not as much.

I thought I was doing pretty well—until Monday, April 24, when I received a phone call from the office of Dick's cardiologist. They had received the official autopsy report. I was prepared to hear that Dick had had a massive heart attack or that the grafts for the arterial bypasses had failed. In a flat, matter-of-fact voice, the nurse said, "It appears that the grafts held and there was no damage to the heart. According to the report, Dick did not have a heart attack. The report did note *severe atherosclerotic disease.* They have ruled this 'an accidental death.'"

My knees wobbled and a cold chill ran through me.

"An accident?" I screamed. "What does that mean—that his death should not have happened, that it could have been prevented?"

The nurse was silent. My head and heart were whirling. I had come so far—and now this. After three months clawing my way out of a nightmare, I finally had a shaky grasp on sanity. With one phone call I lost that fragile foothold.

All night I replayed in my mind the terrible twin days, the 24th of January and the 24th of April. On Tuesday, my friend Lisa brought in lunch for us to share. Before her coat was off, I hugged her desperately. She listened intently as I told her about the phone call. To console me, she said, "Diane, think of this as a good thing. Because you don't have clear-cut answers, it moves you further along on your spiritual path."

On one level, I understood what she meant, but at that moment my spiritual path was far from my mind. I needed real answers about Dick before I could consider my soul. Not knowing was unbearable.

When I spoke to Karen, my sister-in-law, she asked if we should meet with the doctor. Drained from trying to make some sense of all this, I told her I couldn't handle any more right now. I would think it over. By Friday I had spent many sleepless hours trying to decide what to do. I called the doctor. His reaction surprised me.

"I am angry about the autopsy. The coroner only examined the chest area—nothing in the stomach or the head—so we really don't have an answer at all."

I said, "Well, I'm glad for one thing: I'm not angry with you. If it wasn't a heart attack, then no test could have warned you."

The doctor agreed, "I do feel vindicated—but I am not satisfied. It could have been arrhythmia, but Dick had no history of that. Possibly it was a stroke—but because of how the autopsy was done, we will never know."

"Could it have been faulty diving equipment or a leaky oxygen tank?"

"I just don't know enough about diving. At some point we might want to talk to a medical dive expert."

Then the doctor asked me if I wanted a copy of the autopsy report. Without hesitation, I said emphatically, "*No*."

Although I knew that an autopsy had been performed, I had refused to allow myself any mental images. Now the doctor was discussing body areas that had been cut open. *Stop*–this wasn't some TV medical program. This was a man. This was my husband. I hated these discussions. I wanted a one-word explanation for Dick's death, but I never wanted to read the description of what was done in a cold room in Hawaii by some stranger. I never wanted to see the report. I hung up the phone and cried from some very deep place inside me.

On Saturday night I had dinner with Sara. When I told her about the report, she told me that Sid had died of an embolism, the sudden obstruction of a blood vessel. Sara explained that an embolism can occur in many parts of the body, and therefore it was possible that Dick had had an embolism that did not appear in the limited autopsy. Because Sara was a nurse, I listened carefully. I would ask the doctor about this possibility. During dinner Sara carefully turned the conversation to easier topics and I was able to relax for a little while.

On Sunday morning I decided to call Julie, the attorney from Washington who had been diving with Dick. Maybe she could shed some light on this. Julie was shocked to learn about the report. She told me that when Dick was brought to the beach, she overheard someone mention about how much or how little oxygen was left in the tank, but she was not sure what that meant. Was she implying that an improperly prepared tank was possibly to blame?

Like the doctor, Julie was perplexed by the narrow scope of the autopsy. She suggested that we have a forensic pathologist read the report. Perhaps the coroner had a different agenda, like protecting the hotel—or diving and tourism on Maui.

"Are you suggesting a lawsuit?" I asked.

"Not yet." Julie urged me several times to talk with my brother-in-law Leonard, as a family member and as an attorney. I hung up, more confused than before. She had given me food for thought, but who could ever prove either negligence or intent?

On Sunday afternoon, I joined two friends for a performance of *The Magic Flute*. Before the show, I told them of my agony. They were shocked and tried to offer me comfort. I kept saying, "I just don't understand. Dick should be walking around right now."

During a sad part of the opera, when one character sang, "Her heart was breaking of grief," I sobbed silently. At that moment I would have given anything to leap from my seat and run out of the theater. I berated myself for coming. I wasn't ready for crowds of normal people having a lovely Sunday afternoon. I was too deep in my own pain. Then I reminded myself that when I accepted the invitation, I had not yet received the report. At that time, I was "doing better."

On Monday I attended a meeting for a volunteer organization I belonged to. My mind felt like a dry, stretched rubber band, with tiny rips along the edges. Before the meeting I spent a few minutes with my friend Amy, who is a professor of philosophy. She could read the torment in my face. She asked me what was wrong. I told her.

Amy asked me a strange question, "Have you been this angry before?"

Angry? I was taken aback.

"Are you seeing anger? Is that what this is?"

"Absolutely. Anger is a natural part of grieving," she said.

"I guess I haven't felt that one yet."

Amy looked me straight in the eye, "I think you're in denial. I'm glad you're feeling this now. You need to. But tell me, why does this make you angrier than if someone is stricken with cancer?"

Pause. "It just does. Because maybe it didn't need to happen."

We cried together. And indeed, I was very angry. In the afternoon I decided to call Rabbi Silberg, who had often been my rock in difficult times.

"Diane dear, this was a natural disaster, and Dick was a victim of this accident. It is most unlikely that it was anything other than something in his body that caused his death. It was a physical anomaly, completely unavoidable. Until you have more compelling information, this is truly your best answer. You must settle with ambiguity. We all must learn to live with ambiguity. How we handle it is our challenge. Many things in life are without resolution.

"I strongly urge you not to be Sherlock Holmes. You have been compromised by this autopsy. But believe me, Diane, Dick died of natural causes. It could have been a bubble in the brain or in the carotid artery.

"Dick also was completely aware of the risks involved. He knew his physical condition, he knew the risks inherent in this sport, and he loved what he was doing. We all take risks, whether it is riding a bike or driving a car. Even the best of parachuters, experts who hire professionals to pack their chutes, can have something go wrong. They know the risk and they take it. Please, Diane, this is crazy-making. Just let it go."

I listened intently to what the rabbi said. I certainly understood "crazy-making" because that was how it felt—as though my head would burst. Hearing the rabbi's sensitive and sensible ideas gave me some relief from my anguish.

Later that day my brother called. I repeated the whole story to him and mentioned that I was thinking of calling Paulette. Distressed at my distress and unable to help me, David urged me to call her. Just hearing her voice calmed me a little. She truly did not think this was a dive accident. Paulette told me that Dick had finished his work and his lessons on this earth and it was time for him to go on. Toward the end of our conversation I asked what she thought of my calling Laura, Paulette's friend who is a psychic.

Paulette answered, "I have told Laura about our meeting in Hawaii and all that happened. I know she would be happy to talk with you." I took Laura's number, uncertain whether I would use it. I had spoken to so many people— therapist, doctor, lawyer, rabbi, philosopher, family, and friends—grasping for the words that would give me some peace. Could this woman give me a definitive answer? Could I impose on a stranger, by bringing my troubles to her doorstep?

After debating for twenty minutes, I stood up. It was as though my legs walked over to the phone and my fingers dialed. Laura answered. She said she would be glad to try to help me. She asked that I tell her exactly what happened. When I described the past week, I waited through a very long pause. Had I scared her away?

Then with total calm and assurance, she said, "He had an aneurysm." I waited for her to say more. Another long pause. Then she repeated firmly, "He had an aneurysm."

For a long moment, I gulped air. "What is an aneurysm?" I asked.

Laura explained that an aneurysm is a swelling of an artery due to a weakness in its wall, often in the brain or in the aorta. When these burst, death frequently occurs. Atherosclerosis and high blood pressure can cause these ruptures. Without immediate surgical help, chances for survival are slim.

When she finished, I exhaled audibly. It was as though I had been carrying around a huge inflated balloon that suddenly emptied. This explanation made all the sense in the world.

"I'm so glad you have told me this."

"I didn't tell you this to make you glad. I told you because that's what it is. And I get confirmation of that." Laura told me that she had goose bumps and chills on her arm. She added, "Dick is upset because he sees how upset you are." I didn't know how that made me feel. I was beyond holding another emotion.

We talked for another twenty minutes, and I began to feel calm for the first time in a long week.

Later that evening, my brother-in-law Leonard called. With great compassion, he urged me to consider Dick's death b'shert (his time had come, it was meant to be), to stop focusing on the autopsy report, to let it go. He reminded me of the story of Lot's wife, who was turned to stone when she looked back. When I told him about the aneurysm, he agreed that that was perfectly plausible.

When I took my blood pressure that night, it was absolutely normal for the first time in many days. I slept peacefully. The next day at the Grief Group I was able to tell the whole story with serenity and acceptance.

A few days later when I told my stepson Fred about the autopsy report, he was terribly disturbed—so much so that he discussed the circumstances with his rabbi in New Jersey. The rabbi requested a copy of the report, which he then forwarded to his trusted friend, a medical specialist. After studying the report, the doctor responded, "This was the heart attack that was waiting to happen. It was inevitable, considering Dick's condition. It was a different kind of heart attack, one that would not show up in the autopsy that was conducted." Fred was satisfied with this opinion, and I was glad for that.

On Friday morning of that dreadful week, as I was beginning to pull myself together, I received a carton from the Maui police department—all Dick's scuba gear. The UPS man read the label and looked at me quizzically. I could not speak, much less answer his unasked question. My hands shook as I signed the register. I picked up the carton and carried it down the steps to the basement. I could not bring myself to open it.

One sunny day in July, I went into the basement with a knife and a clipboard. The owner of Dick's favorite dive shop had urged me to take an inventory of all the scuba gear. He would be happy to try to dispose of it for me. I opened the box.

One by one I pulled out the sandy relics of that day in Hawaii—the regulator, the dive computer, the fins, the buoyancy compensatory, the tubes that carried oxygen, the dive knife, the writing board—all the equipment Dick was wearing so confidently when he entered the water on January 24. I touched each and every piece, hoping for some answer or consolation. But metal, rubber, and nylon gave me neither. I cried a little. Hastily, I scribbled down the inventory and repacked the box, glad that the task I had put off for so long was now complete. I climbed back upstairs and went out into the sunshine, sat on the porch, and sobbed.

During the first three months after Dick's death, I had moved through the normal, early phases of grief, and I had begun to put together the pieces of my life. That week hurled me back into the acute state of grief. Because by then I was past the initial shock, the impact was enormous. Furthermore, the close, daily support of friends and family was no longer there. People had gone on with their lives. In April I was much more alone.

Maybe everyone who loses a loved one has his own battery of terrible questions, the *Why's, What if's,* and *If only's.* For me it was the new questions raised three months later that nearly broke me. Over the next few months, these questions fell into two camps, rational and philosophical. The first set dealt with Dick's medical history and care, with the dive itself, and with the autopsy.

Why hadn't Dick listened to the warnings of doctors? Had he employed "magical thinking," believing that no harm could befall him? Could or should I have been stronger in urging Dick not to dive? Would he have listened? Would some medical test have revealed an impending aneurysm or embolism?

Was the dive conducted properly? Were the tanks properly filled and functioning? Why was the dive guide the first one out of the water? Other divers told me that the guide should always be last, watching and guiding his clients. Would the guide have noticed that something was wrong? If he had reached Dick sooner, would quicker medical attention have saved his life?

And why did we need an autopsy at all? Hawaiian law requires an autopsy for a sudden death; strict Jewish law prohibits it. Should I have protested more strongly on religious grounds? Why did it take so long to get the report? Why didn't the coroner examine above and below the heart area? Why did he use the words *accidental death*?

For a brief moment, in the anger evoked by all these questions, I considered a lawsuit—but against whom? Very quickly, I knew that I had neither the desire nor the energy to extend my own torture. And to what end? It wouldn't bring Dick back, and it would surely bring me down. In the end, it all came down to one question: If any one of these elements had been different, would Dick have survived? I would never know.

Sara, a nurse, had offered me the first acceptable medical possibility. Laura, a psychic, gave me the answer that set me free, the answer that I clung to, not only because it made sense—doctors confirmed that an aneurysm was a strong possibility—but also because it allowed me to let go of all the other medical questions.

The second set of questions arose from my need to find some meaning in that week of torment. Was I being tested for some existential purpose? What did I need to learn or gain? Did I become more enlightened?

As I looked back and thought of those who tried to help me, I realized that each person I turned to in my agony gave me wisdom. Only much later did I put it all together and realize that each and every answer was the right answer. Each answer was a gift. Amy, the philosopher, had helped me to acknowledge and eventually move past my anger. Leonard's story about Lot's wife gave exactly the same message. Paulette told me that Dick had completed his mission on this earth. Most days I could accept that. The rabbi had told me that we must all learn to live with ambiguity—how difficult that is, especially in a matter of life and death. But I was learning.

My friend Lisa had told me that I could now go forward on my own spiritual path. Maybe soon I would be ready for that, one slow step at a time.

Many times in the months that followed, all the questions of that awful week would resurface, and I would cry out, "Yes, but . . ." and slide back into the mire of questions. Then, when I realized the direction I was going, I would try to ground myself by repeating the Serenity Prayer: "*God, grant me the serenity to accept the things I cannot change, the courage to change the things I can, and the wisdom to know the difference*" [1].

What was the choice?

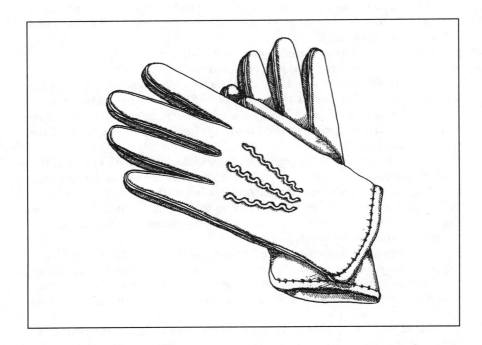

CHAPTER 7

A Pair of Gloves

"It is possible to live a good, full life, a very satisfying life, to enjoy your activities, have fun, to be with friends you like. I am proud of myself. Given what I've gone through in my life, I'm fairly sane, managing just fine. I think I've done better than a lot of people would have done." These words and a warm smile were my introduction to Eliana Michael, a woman whose journey would move me to tears many times over the next few hours.

Eliana is a bright-eyed, attractive woman of 61 who looks ten years younger. Her dark pixie hair and neat figure belie a mother of four, grandmother of five. But then, she had an early start.

In the summer of 1957, Eliana met Elliott Michael on a blind date, an evening she recalls in detail. At 25, Elliott seemed an "older man" to Eliana who at 20 was a rising junior in college. On the first date, Elliott took her to an outdoor concert and to a special Chinese restaurant. He was quite taken with her and asked her out for a second date. When Eliana returned from a family vacation, she saw Elliott again. On the third date he proposed.

"I just looked at him and said, 'Are you crazy or what? I hardly know you!' We agreed to date and see how it went. He was in earnest in his search for a wife. We were engaged at Thanksgiving and married the following April." Because Eliana was getting married, she decided to leave school. She had been studying elementary education.

"I told Elliott he saved a lot of kids from me and me from them. I love kids, especially my own, but not 25 in a classroom!"

After Elliott and Eliana married, Elliott wanted children immediately. When no pregnancy occurred, they adopted their daughter Roberta. Eliana was 22 at the time. Nineteen years later, Roberta married and had her first daughter at 20, making Eliana a grandmother at 42. After Roberta, the Michaels adopted two boys, and then Eliana gave birth to their daughter Barbara. The family now had four children, a large home, and a secure income.

Elliott graduated from college with a Bachelor of Science in Economics. After a stint in the service, he returned home and went to work in his family's jewelry store. After fifteen years, Elliott left the business and entered a field that always greatly interested him. He became a stockbroker, working for a national brokerage firm. From now on his income would be based on production. Leaving the security of the jewelry store was a risk the couple was willing to take.

"Elliott loved his work. He was a very conservative person, and that's the way he handled clients' money, never churning accounts. Eventually he became a vice-president of the company. He took a great deal of pride in his work," said Eliana with pride of her own.

His clients appreciated Elliott. "One day the doorbell rang, and there was a florist delivering the most beautiful bone china bowl with a gorgeous array of flowers. Enclosed was a card from a client to me, 'Thank you for having such a wonderful husband.'"

Sometimes clients would call Elliott with the latest stock tip. He would check it out, and if he didn't consider it wise, he would tell the client, "My advice is take the money and go to Las Vegas. You'll have more fun losing it that way." Eliana smiled, recalling Elliott's gentle humor and his integrity.

Eliana took a deep breath, as though contemplating a dive into icy water. When she spoke again, the tone of her voice was different, stretched taut over her words. Her speech became terse, staccato. She sat up straight as she began the chronology of Elliott's illness and reported with accuracy, and even some detachment, the course of their lives.

FEBRUARY 1981–MAY 1982

In February 1981, Elliott and Eliana planned their first trip to Israel. In December Elliott had complained of rectal pain. When Eliana urged him to see a doctor, he declined. It would go away. When the pain persisted, she pointed out that they would be walking a lot on their trip, so Elliott went to a proctologist to check out his problem.

Alarmed by what he saw, the doctor sent Elliott to the hospital for a complete work-up. Tests revealed that all of Elliott's organs were being forced into wrong places inside him, and this pressure was causing the pain. Further tests revealed a tumor. When Eliana arrived at the hospital to learn the results, Elliott told her, "They're sending me to New York for surgery—I think to Sloan-Kettering."

Eliana said, "But you don't have cancer."

The surgeon came in and closed the door. "This is not good. You have a tumor, and we don't know if it is cancer. There's a surgeon in New York who is known for getting in and out of that area of the body with minimal negatives. I have called him to schedule the surgery. Your airplane arrangements are made too. You're going tonight."

Stunned, Eliana went home and mechanically packed their bags. Her mother came to stay with the two children still living at home. Elliott's uncle drove them to the airport. He asked Eliana, "How much money do you have?"

"About $30," answered Eliana. Who was thinking about money? The man emptied his pockets and Eliana and Elliott flew to New York with about $100. They took a cab to the hospital and Elliott checked into his room.

"What am I supposed to do now, Elliott?" asked Eliana.

"Guess you'd better get a hotel room," he answered. Somehow Eliana finally found a hotel but how would she pay? The Michaels had just decided to cut up their credit cards and make purchases by cash or check. So there she was, in New York City, with no credit card and a few dollars. She paid for one night. The next day she set out to find a bank and cash a check.

"Sorry, we can't cash an out-of-state check," said the teller.

"Call my bank," Eliana said desperately.

"We can't do that," said the teller. Even under the stress she was feeling about Elliott, Eliana handled the situation with equanimity. She called a cousin who lived in New York. Within a few hours, the cousin came by with $200.

The complex operation was performed several days later. Because of the location of the tumor, two teams worked on Elliott, front and back. Finally the doctors announced that the surgery was very successful, and the tumor was removed. Benign. Elliott and Eliana were ecstatic with relief. They had dodged a bullet. Life would go on.

Several days later, when it was time to remove the stitches and staples, Eliana sat calmly in the waiting room. Soon Elliott would be released and they could go home. When the doctor called her into the office to join them, Elliott said quietly, "Doctor, tell her what you told me about the report." Eliana could not imagine what was coming.

"We must reclassify the tumor as a sarcoma. It is mildly malignant, meaning six cells in 1000 are malignant. Because the tumor is encapsulated, we are hopeful that it won't spread. Still you will need to watch this very carefully," the doctor reported in a flat, matter-of-fact tone.

"He was gruff, not kind or reassuring at all," Eliana's face tightened as she remembered hearing the fatal words. "I felt like my heart was breaking inside me, like somebody kicked me. I couldn't catch my breath. We returned to Elliott's room, not saying much. This was the first and last time I broke down. I sat in the bathroom and cried. I was devastated. Two days later we returned to the doctor for removal of the last stitches. I told the doctor how upset I was by his chilly pronouncement."

"Why is that?" asked the doctor, puzzled.

"You told me my husband has cancer," she said emotionally.

"I can't help that," he responded.

That a doctor could be so cold, so callous was incomprehensible. If he had taken his sharpest surgical blade and pierced her heart, it could not have hurt more.

When Elliott's sister called, he instructed Eliana not to tell anyone.

Sparing the family took a toll on Eliana. "Keeping Elliott's illness a secret was his idea. At that time we were very optimistic. His feeling was why worry other people? We didn't even tell the children. Had it been my decision, I would have told. I am a very open, honest person, not deceptive, so it was very hard for me to keep the secret. It felt like a lie. When anyone asked about Elliott, I said that he needed to be checked regularly. This deception was very hard on me. Telling would have been easier. And besides, we needed support. But that was the way he wanted it, and I respected his decision."

The family picked up their lives. Then in July, Elliott returned from a tennis match limping badly. He had twisted his ankle, which was now huge and purple. When Elliott next visited the doctor, the lymph node in his ankle was badly swollen, a condition that the orthopedist assumed was caused by the leg injury.

It was time for Elliott's six-month appointment in New York. The surgeon became alarmed by the ankle and ordered Elliott to return home for a biopsy immediately.

The internist had more bad news.

"The malignancy has spread to the lymph system. I've called in an oncologist. Elliott will need CAT scans every three months."

Elliott's doctors did not recommend chemotherapy because there was no visible tumor, which meant that there was no way to measure the effectiveness of the drugs. The doctors hoped that the cancer was confined to that one node in his ankle, which had been removed during the biopsy. Elliott was sent home to recover.

Eliana's parents had been at the hospital for the biopsy procedure and were aware of the results. Recognizing now that Elliott's illness was progressing, the Michaels decided it was appropriate to share the entire situation with their children, their families, and their friends.

For Eliana it was a relief when people knew. She and Elliott were glad for the support and encouragement because they had felt so alone for all those months. Eliana said, "It was so much easier not to handle it alone. My mother-in-law berated me, not for keeping the secret but for going through it all alone. In retrospect I know she was right."

It was now fall 1981. Confused by the diagnosis, the Michaels decided to visit the Mayo Clinic. The Mayo opinion was that, for this kind of cancer, if any further cancer appeared, cold, hard steel—surgery—was the best option. They explained that chemotherapy can stop the cancer but it will recur. Elliott's cancer was virulent; the Mayo opinion was prophetic.

Eliana's heart sank; her optimism wavered. "This was the moment that I said to myself, 'Maybe this isn't going to turn out as I had hoped.'"

From the fall of 1981 to spring of 1982, Elliott seemed to be doing well. He worked and led an almost normal life, but always the cloud of fear hung over him.

In May 1982, the doctors found a tumor in Elliott's lung. For two days he was prepped for thoracic surgery. Just before the surgery, a routine CAT scan revealed cancer in the liver, a blood-rich organ and thus a favorite site for sarcomas. The doctors scrapped the surgery and recommended chemotherapy. This disease was relentless.

The oncologist said, "If you are willing to go elsewhere, it is time to go. This is a most unusual case."

In June, marshalling more strength, Eliana and Elliott were on their way to M.D. Anderson Cancer Center in Houston, Texas. When they arrived, they met their doctor, a Greek man with a very thick accent, difficult to understand.

Eliana's first reaction was, "Dear God, why do you always do this to us?" She was angry. "But we soon learned that God had taken good care of us. This doctor was very bright, encouraging, uplifting, and he really liked us. At one point he said that he really admired us."

"We have no choice," responded Eliana. "You're keeping Elliott alive."

The first trip to Houston cost well over $1000, a very large sum in 1982. After that first trip, Elliott's company paid for the Michaels' airfare and hotels for every visit, which in six years totaled more than fifty trips. "I will always be grateful for that generosity and for the relief from financial pressure. And what a tremendous tribute that was to Elliott," she added proudly.

The trips were arduous, stressful, and exhausting. Sometimes Elliott took chemotherapy treatments locally, but Anderson was more aggressive and gave higher doses of the powerful drugs.

Eliana smiled as she described the better times. "We'd come home and it was like heaven. We just wanted to go back to our normal lives, friends, and family. Then about a week before each trip, the tension, dread, and fear mounted. The worst part was the uncertainty. Is this treatment going to work or is it not? We never had peace. Once Elliott had the tests, at least we knew what was happening. It was the unknown that was so hard. It was like a roller-coaster ride – good news, bad news, new treatment, more doctors, more opinions, and always physical pain for Elliott. My job was to hold myself together and be strong for him."

Between trips Elliott continued to work, which was his salvation. "He had amazing strength to keep going, to endure all that he did," said Eliana.

Eliana continued her own work as part-time bookkeeper and secretary in an art gallery that presented shows of local artists. "I'm strong. I was always strong, and that held me in good stead. I never sat down. I was extremely energized. I just kept going."

FALL 1984–DECEMBER 1987

The chemotherapy treatments which began in 1982 in Houston were effective for about two years. The tumors in Elliott's liver and lungs shrank. Then Elliott underwent two surgeries, the first in the fall of 1984 to remove the residual tumors from his liver. The following spring, more surgery removed the remaining tumors from his lungs. Tumors in both areas were now 98 percent necrotic, dead. That was good news. Once again they had hope.

A month after the second surgery, Eliana put her arms around Elliott and felt a bulge behind his armpit. Another tumor. Once again Elliott had surgery and was then placed on chemotherapy, this time for two years, from 1985 to 1987.

JANUARY 1988–NOVEMBER 1991

"In 1988 things really went sour," explained Eliana. "Tumors appeared on Elliott's head, over his eye, behind his ears, like little marbles. They were very disfiguring.

"By the spring the Houston team ran out of their bag of tricks." They could offer experimental drugs, but that would mean the Michaels would have to relocate to Houston for daily treatment. They decided against moving. Instead they went to the University of Wisconsin Hospital in Madison, to the head of the sarcoma department, who advised surgery to get rid of the obvious tumors. The surgery was terrible, and afterward Eliana had to change the dressings twice a day. Elliott was in great pain. Finally he began to recover.

Then one night in June, Elliott turned over in bed and broke his hip. Surgery was required to repair the damage. Finally, after excruciating, prolonged pain, Elliott came home from the hospital and began to mend. Amazingly, he returned to work part time. In July, Elliott was best man in Eliana's brother's wedding. He had never been a best man, and he was thrilled.

By Labor Day weekend of 1988, Elliott felt sick and miserable. He went to the hospital in Madison for five days, where he attended a support group for people who were dying. These sessions upset him deeply. After valiantly fighting his way through the minefield of cancer treatments, Elliott was facing the end of his journey, and he was afraid.

"In the past, we always held out the hope of a new medication, breakthroughs in medical journals," said Eliana. "We had trouble believing that the worst could happen. We had allowed ourselves to be lulled into a sense of security. We thought there would always be another treatment. And that had kept us going."

Two weeks later a chest x-ray revealed multiple tumors in Elliott's lungs. Elliott remained in the hospital until the end of September, when the doctors finally told him, "There is nothing more we can do but keep you comfortable."

Elliott wanted to go home to die.

"I was scared to death," Eliana recalled. "I hadn't cried very much, since the diagnosis in New York. I just kept going and doing, hoping that we could save Elliott's life."

Never cried? An eight-year cycle of life in the stark world of cancer— shock, tests, relief, bad diagnoses, hospitals, encouragement, despair, compassion, dispassion, indifference, hope, surgeries, drugs—would have exhausted and decimated most people. Eliana never cried.

At the end Elliott suffered a lot mentally because he was afraid, knowing that he was going to die. He had all his mental faculties. How could he not know? The rabbi came and talked to him; the cantor came with his guitar and sang.

A nurse from hospice came to visit. For the first time Eliana was able to open up and express her feelings.

"I had been upset that my faith had no comfort to offer me in facing Elliott's death. I told the nurse how I envied the comfort that Catholic people find in their faith. Her answer surprised me. 'Don't kid yourself. Many Catholics suffer just as you are. We are afraid too.'"

Eliana felt a peculiar relief to learn that suffering and the fear of death are universal, that even the most devout are not spared.

The visitor who most comforted Elliott was a rabbi who was a hospital chaplain and the author of a book on death and grieving. He came to the house a few days before Thanksgiving.

"I didn't hear all that the chaplain said, but I was in the next room and heard part of it. Elliott said that he didn't know what to expect. The chaplain painted a picture of God on His throne. 'You'll come before Him, and He will ask your Hebrew name. Then you will talk about your life. You will be in a good place. You've had your hell here on earth.' The rabbi's words relaxed and comforted Elliott, and for that I was grateful. That visit made all the difference. It gave Elliott the serenity that he had been seeking, and that I wanted for him. It allowed him to die peacefully."

Elliott passed away the Tuesday before Thanksgiving. Eliana was with him. "He just stopped breathing. I remember thinking, 'After all this time, all this struggle, this is how it ends.' It was very peaceful."

The day after the funeral one of Eliana's closest friends came over and they sat on the couch. Taking Eliana's hand, Kathy said, "There is something I want to tell you, and I hope it won't be upsetting for you."

In a low voice Kathy told Eliana that in the middle of the night, she sensed someone's presence in the dark room. It was Elliott. He spoke, "Tell Eliana I'm okay."

Eliana jumped up and began to cry.

"When I calmed down, she repeated the story. You know, I did believe this. Kathy is the one person he would come to. She is solid as a rock, and she was very definite. The message was very clear, 'Tell her I'm okay.' It gave me some comfort. I know he was there. I wish he would come to me now."

At the time of Elliott's death, a nurse had praised Eliana's strength, "You're really taking this well."

"I think that was because I had no emotions left," explained Eliana.

When her daughter Barbara came home for the funeral on Thanksgiving Day, Eliana hugged her, dry-eyed. "I fought tears. How stupid of me—I didn't want her to see me cry. To this day I have never had a good cry. The only times I cried were at the funeral and when friends and family called on the phone. At times I became teary, but I never had a down-and-out cry."

Most women speak of uncontrollable tears and sudden outbursts during their husbands' illnesses and after their deaths. Crying is a kind of catharsis. Most people say that they needed to cry and that they usually felt better afterward. How could one lose a spouse and not cry? How dreadful to carry around that mass of pain and grief and never let it out. Somewhere I read that the chemical composition of tears shed in sorrow is different from any other kind. Tears of grief physically clean out toxins and help release pain. Eliana never had that release.

Six weeks before Elliott's death Eliana began to see a counselor. "After Elliott died, I became reliant on a therapist who perhaps did more harm than good. Each week I felt worse. I didn't understand why we were talking about when I was five. What she did with me was wrong. Foolishly, I continued seeing her for close to three years, and I was going down, down, down.

"Finally, when I was unable to sleep past 3:30 A.M., I went to a neurologist, the head of a sleep clinic, who told me that the only reason for my sleep problem was depression. He wanted me to go to a psychiatrist for medication. I was scared of doing that. Instead I stayed with my therapist, and I never shed a tear. I even tried to cry by looking at old photos and listening to tapes of Elliott's voice. I just held it all in."

In the three years after Elliott's death, Eliana became less and less functional. She slept only three hours a night. She couldn't go to the grocery store or cook a meal; she couldn't make plans for herself. It was as though she was paralyzed. The only place she could function was at work at the gallery, with its emotionless structure and routine.

DECEMBER 1991–DECEMBER 1999

At Chanukah of 1991, Eliana went shopping in a department store to purchase gloves for one daughter's husband and the other daughter's boyfriend. "I spent an hour picking up a pair of gloves and then putting them back. I couldn't make a decision. I was in a terrible state. Standing there in front of that glove counter, I suddenly realized that I was falling apart. I knew I had to do something to save myself."

She canceled all her future appointments with the therapist and called a psychiatrist. Eliana's first question to the doctor was, "Must we start from age 2?"

The woman's compassionate voice quelled her fears. "No, we do not need to go back to your childhood. Any concerns there will come out. You had a happy childhood, good parents. You were lucky." Feeling encouragement and hope, Eliana scheduled her first appointment.

Eliana continued with this doctor for the next eight years. With time, therapy, and medication, she has worked through a great deal.

"Nobody has to live in that kind of misery forever. My mistake was holding myself together all those years. I should have gone for help during all the years that Elliott was sick, but I wasn't thinking about me then. I came close to a breakdown. I wish I'd gone to a psychiatrist at the beginning. I had misplaced loyalty and that hurt me. I have a history of depression, a biological predisposition to it. I also have SAD, Seasonal Affect Disorder. When the weather is gloomy, I am too. I am on a new medication to help with that. Now I can concentrate, I can sleep well. I'll probably be on medication forever, and that is fine with me."

What is the impact of a long illness on the survivor? Eliana believes that the longer the illness, the care-giving, and the medical nightmare, the longer the recovery time for the survivor. "Elliott was ill for eight years—an extra five easily, due to the Houston treatments—but he often said his illness was harder on me."

Eliana believes that the effect on the family of a lengthy illness is immeasurable. The spouse and other family members may require professional help in facing all the years of sickness and then the death of the loved one.

In 1992, Eliana sold her house and moved into an apartment. Five years later, she purchased a condo. She gutted the kitchen and bathroom, carpeted, painted, and worked with a decorator to create the feeling of home. She chose wonderful plants and lovely artwork. The light, happy side of Eliana shines in her home, and she loves every square inch. The cheerful room where we sat would never reveal that its creator had suffered such desolation, such prolonged and terrible grief.

"It has been a long road for me. What I know now is that the grieving process, which really begins during the illness, may require medical help and psychotherapy. The length of the illness and all those trips were the hardest part. Although I did grow stronger over those years, I know that if I had gone for help sooner, and had found the right person, I would be farther along today. We can change, but we need guidance and support. I really needed to cry for such a long time. No one has to tough it out alone. It doesn't take anything away from the sick person to take care of yourself. I wish I had sought out professional help during those dreadful years. I guess taking care of me was far from my mind then. In my effort to be selfless, I paid a heavy price."

After a moment Eliana smiled softly, looked around her lovely home, sighed wistfully and said, "When I look at myself today, I say 'Thank God I got help.' At last I have a good, full life which is very satisfying. I have fun with my friends, I travel, I enjoy my activities. Truly, I have a fine life."

She chuckled quietly, "And thank God for those gloves!"

CHAPTER 8

Dinner for Ten

It was Saturday, May 21, 6:15 P.M. The dinner guests would be arriving shortly. I adjusted the flower arrangement about five degrees. Then I stood back and admired the flowers I had added to bring a touch of spring to the setting. Was it possible that barely four months after Dick's death, I was having ten people to my home for dinner?

Soon after Dick died, I learned that for women who are alone, Saturday nights required special attention. What had been "date night" in college and "couples night" for the next thirty or forty years now carried an extra edge of loneliness for women alone. To insure against those lonely evenings, several members of the Grief Group and a few other widows had come together to form a loose but loyal social group whose single status bound them together. In two's, three's, or more, they made plans for weekends, especially Saturday nights. Everyone was welcome to join the group, whatever the activity.

Now, two months later, I tensed as I recalled my first outing with the group. One Saturday night in March, I was invited to join several women for dinner at an Italian restaurant. The picture unreeled in my mind: a large room with a high beamed ceiling, wooden tables, bottles of wine, convivial laughter, and conversation. The women were bright, vivacious, interesting.

Why had that evening been so painful for me? In my mind's eye, I saw the restaurant filled with couples out on a Saturday night—man, woman, boy, girl— and one table of seven attractive, well-dressed, middle-aged women. I was now part of that group endeavor, carefully selecting the toppings for a pizza, scrupulously divvying up the slices, and meticulously measuring out the two bottles of wine. Then it was time to find a calculator, tally up the bill, divide by seven, figure out the tip, add that in. I watched seven wallets emerging from seven purses, three people needing change, and dollars piling up in the center of the table.

It had seemed so easy and natural for the six of them. As far as I could tell, they were oblivious to all the couples. But then, I was the novice, the new widow, and this was not yet my milieu. I was still accustomed to being with my husband on Saturday night. Many of them had been alone for a year or two or more. I knew I would learn to be comfortable in this situation, but that night was a painful reminder of what had been and what would be.

The first week in May, Shari and I had planned to go out for dinner on Saturday night. "Shari, do you think we could have dinner at my house on Saturday? At this point I am so much happier at home. I don't feel the need to be out. I would rather be at home, and I'm happy to cook. Would you mind?"

Without hesitation, Shari responded, "I understand perfectly. Sometimes I get so tired of going out. Why don't I bring a fruit salad?"

The tension left my shoulders and relief rolled in. "Thank you. I'll really look forward to that. Do you think Naomi and Sara are available?"

They were both delighted. Naomi said, "That sounds so lovely. You know, I had a call today from Eliana, and she wanted to make plans too. Do you think...?"

So it began. Within a few days, we were up to seven people. I was amazed how quickly the evening came together and even more that each guest seemed so genuinely pleased, so happy to be invited to my home. At least three said, "Great! Sure beats another restaurant!" Did I detect some special electricity of excitement, or was I projecting my own feelings?

In my nightly chats with Dick, I told him about the dinner. In my mind I felt his encouragement, although I also caught myself wondering if such a festivity so early in my grieving seemed inappropriate.

"This is not a party," I told Dick and myself. "Just a group of women getting together for dinner at our house." I heard him cheer me on, "Go for it, Sweetie!"

By Wednesday the meal chart was complete. I carefully insured that the menu wouldn't turn out to be five salads and no hors d'ouevres, vegetables, or dessert. When I realized that we had no real entrée, I decided to serve Israeli chicken, which was embarrassingly simple to prepare but looked fancy and even a little exotic.

By Wednesday I had developed the same case of "party nerves" I always had when entertaining. But this would be different—an audience of ladies who had all given many dinner parties. I cleaned and straightened, carefully planned and arranged the silver and china, and ordered a centerpiece. Everything was falling into place and the anticipation gave me unexpected purpose and pleasure.

Late Thursday evening I finally settled down to read. At ten o'clock the phone rang. I jumped. Who would call so late?

My son Bruce was calling from New York. "Mom, it's me. More bad news."

My heart stopped. "What is it, sweetheart?"

"Dad died." And he began to sob. I was too startled to utter a word. Finally Bruce was able to speak, "At about seven tonight he had a massive heart attack."

On Friday morning, I called the nine guests to postpone the dinner by two weeks, for May 21. On Saturday morning, Margie and I were on a plane to Pennsylvania for the funeral of the man I had loved at 16, married at 21, divorced at 40, and had seen last at Bruce's wedding the previous March. Jake had looked old and weary. Time, stress, and chronic health problems had taken their toll. But the man had just turned 60. What was happening in this world, in my world?

My own acute pain was so recent that I could almost feel the waves of shock that were surging through my daughter. Over time Margie had made peace with her Dad's distance over the last 20 years. As we waited through long delays in two airports and then sat on two crowded airplanes, her pale blue eyes filled up with tears every few minutes. Sometimes she wept uncontrollably, wiping away the long, blond curls that fell into her face. At times I cried with her, as I held her and let her cry.

I felt the same helplessness that all witnesses to grief feel. I tried my best to comfort Margie, telling her how much her dad and I loved her. "And I'm not going anywhere, my sweetheart. I'll always be here with you." I felt instinctively the need to reassure my child, a child who had now lost two fathers in four months.

In Pennsylvania, I faced another funereal tableau. Jake's older brother, a recent widower, was shaken by yet another untimely loss. Jake's cousins, losing their first familial contemporary, shared their childhood memories of the time when their three families grew up together and Jake was "the little *mazik*," the mischievous little boy. My heart ached for my children, so full of tangled memories, regrets, and sadness for all the time they and their Dad had missed and would never have.

Sue, Jake's sweetheart of 17 years, was in a state of shock and ripped apart by a pain almost beyond endurance. We talked a little, cried together, and she accepted whatever comfort I could give her. Because my own loss was so recent and so similar, I tried to offer Sue the understanding that few others could. In a way, it was confusing to be the one giving support. Was I now the veteran? I promised to be in touch with her soon.

Somehow the weekend passed, and I was relieved to be going home, back to what had now become my normal life. Over the next week I tried to comfort and support the children. But I understood too well that they would have to face loss in their own way.

By the following Monday, I was able to gear up for the dinner. I was happy for the diversion. Three more women were available for the new date. Renee knew none of the other women, and I was happy that she could come. Peggy, a Southern friend, was delighted. Joan, a woman of great wit, would be a fine addition.

On Thursday I cleaned the house and prepared the food. On Friday I polished silver, set the table, pulled some weeds, and swept the walk. The house and yard looked their best, as if they wanted to shine for my new friends. On Saturday I purchased wine. At 3:30 P.M., I put the ingredients in the bread machine. By 5 o'clock the aroma of Italian herb bread permeated the house.

The guests began arriving at 6:30, all armed with carefully prepared and arranged bowls, pans, or platters of food. The buffet in the dining room filled with colorful and tantalizing food. Everyone had gone all out. The food was a great success, and I saw people going back for seconds. The *piece de resistance* were the desserts.

The house filled with laughter and chatter. I heard people introducing themselves to other people. During the evening, several stories caused downright hilarity. I caught bits of conversations around the table: trips taken or planned, books, theater, movies, jobs, amusing experiences. As I looked around at these articulate, accomplished women, I was delighted.

As the evening progressed, it was apparent that my guests were comfortable and happy. They were having fun! The group stayed late, a sure sign of a good party. The second sign was how much I as the hostess enjoyed the evening. Lavish and enthusiastic praise for the idea echoed around me. When one guest asked for the phone list so that she could invite the group to her home for a future gathering, I was delighted.

After the last guest left, and the kitchen was acceptable, I fell into bed, exhausted but exhilarated. Almost asleep, I suddenly had a bittersweet moment. Certainly the dinner had been a success by any measure and a real high for me, but now I had no one with whom to share it. Where was Dick for our post-party "debriefing"? I needed to tell him how proud and pleased I felt.

I sighed, closed my eyes, and began talking. "Ricardo," I said, using my pet name for Dick, "What a night this was! Everybody loved our house, the food was great, and we all had a wonderful time. And did you see that plum dessert? You would have loved it."

An animated monologue tumbled out as I told Dick all about the evening. I knew he was listening and grinning. I heard my voice, his words, "I knew you could do it. Sweetie, I'm so proud of you!"

That night I slept very well.

⠀⠀⠀⠀⠀⠀⠀⠀cß　　cß　　cß

ISRAELI CHICKEN

4-6 chicken breasts: oil and brown in hot oven or broil.

Sauce:
1 small can frozen OJ diluted to 8 oz.
1 small jar stuffed olives
1 can pitted ripe olives
1 medium onion sliced in rings
1 T. brown sugar
¼ c. olive oil
1 t. thyme
1 t. paprika, dash salt

Simmer sauce 4 minutes and pour over chicken. Bake at 350 for 1¾ hours, basting often. Serve with rice.

RAMONA'S PLUM TART

Crust:
1 cup unbleached all-purpose flour
3 tablespoons sugar
½ cup (1 stick) chilled unsalted butter, cut into pieces
½ teaspoon salt
2 large egg yolks, beaten to blend

Combine first 3 ingredients in bowl; stir to blend.

Add butter and cut in, using pastry blender or fingertips until mixture resembles coarse meal. Add yolks.

Stir with fork until moist clumps form. Gather dough into ball; flatten into disk.

Wrap dough in plastic, chill until firm, about 30 minutes.

Can be made 3 days ahead. Keep chilled. Let soften slightly at room temperature before using.

Tart:
Butter
7 large red plums, pitted, each cut into 8 wedges
4 tablespoons sugar
½ teaspoon ground cinnamon
1 egg white, beaten to blend
vanilla ice cream

Preheat oven to 400 degrees. Line baking sheet with foil; butter foil. Place plums on prepared sheet, spacing evenly. Sprinkle with 2T. sugar. Bake until plums are tender but still hold shape, about 30 minutes.

Roll out dough on floured surface to a circle with 12-inch diameter.

Transfer pastry to center of another large, heavy baking sheet. Overlap plums in concentric circles on pastry, forming 9-inch circle in the center.

Combine remaining 2T. sugar and cinnamon in small bowl. Sprinkle sugar mixture over plums. Fold edge of pastry over plums, pinching to seal any cracks in pastry. Brush crust twice with egg white.

Bake tart until crust is golden, about 25 minutes.

Run thin, sharp knife carefully under tart edges to loosen from sheet. Cool 15 to 35 minutes. Serve slightly warm with vanilla ice cream.

Note: This recipe works equally well with kiwi, peaches, and apricots.

One of the men took this picture at the Henry's Fork.
Look closely and you can see the double rainbow.

CHAPTER 9

The Hatchmatcher and the Rainbow

I have known Kay Johnson for about 15 years. A friend of a friend, she became my Shaklee lady and has kept me in healthy vitamins and information for a long time. Now in her late sixties, Kay lost her husband Doug sixteen years ago.

Kay's youthful appearance and energy have always amazed me, and I have admired her bright blue eyes, wide smile, and buoyant enjoyment of life. Compassionate and warm, she is always honest and never a Pollyanna. It is impossible to be with her and feel sad.

When Dick died, Kay was the first person who came to see me. She let me cry, then spent exactly the right length of time and words with me. She called often, always upbeat but never forced or frivolous. When I was suffering, Kay offered sympathy laced with comforting support that came from the wisdom of experience.

During the next few months we spoke on the phone, went to the Imax, shared meals. Kay's broad interests included the stock market, health and wellness, exercise, gardening, travel, and her five little granddaughters. She was always energetic, interesting, and fun to be with.

Sometimes I was taken aback by the directness and strength that came from this gentle woman.

One day over coffee, I commented, "I feel so diminished by Dick's death. Sometimes I wonder about my own identity," I sighed, waiting for her to sigh and say, "I know. I felt the same way."

Instead, I heard, "You are Diane Kaimann and *you* are all you need. You are a fine, competent, complete, wonderful person in your own right. Never even consider that you are any less a person than you were before." The tone of her voice and the intensity of her statement jolted me. My self-deprecating observation was nothing more than self-pity. I knew that Kay was right: who I was had not changed. I sat up a little taller. I needed to remember this when my self-esteem flagged, as it often did these days.

One night we discussed the course of grieving, how it is different for each person. Kay said, "Diane, I have a friend who lost her husband ten years ago, and she is still depressed. Everything in her life is sad. She is really mad with her husband for leaving her alone and she's always complaining about that. Life is so full of excitement and beauty. There was a reason why Doug left and I am here, and I want to live and enjoy all that I can."

Then she asked, "Did I tell you what happened the first time someone referred to me as a widow? I looked her straight in the eye and I practically throttled her. 'I am NOT a widow! I am Kay Johnson. I am my own person. Don't ever use that word around me again!'"

I felt a silent cheer go up inside. I too had avoided the word, even in my thoughts. I would look in the mirror and say, "You don't *look* like a widow. Widows are sad, pathetic, lonely, and old!" Once again, Kay had zeroed in on a painful aspect of my new life and turned it into a strong statement of confidence and optimism.

As the weeks turned into months, I continued to see Kay often. In early June we planned to spend the next Saturday together. It was the night before Father's Day and a beautiful evening. After a quiet dinner, we walked for a few minutes. Then we returned to my house, where Kay admired all the flowers and the work I had done. It had been a pleasant time. We discussed investments and books we had read. Suddenly tired, I yawned and noted that it was 9 P.M. I was ready to call it a night.

When we walked into the family room, Kay admired a crystal spider on a table. "I love crystals," she commented. "I have several in my house. They create the most beautiful rainbows. I just love rainbows. If you hang this near some light, you will have a rainbow."

A unique interest, I thought vaguely, and odd too. Just that morning I had attended a class in Feng Shui, where the instructor had discussed crystals and had shown how they collect light and distribute good *chi*, positive energy, through the colorful rainbows they create. And now here was Kay, ten hours later, talking about crystals and rainbows.

Suddenly, from nowhere, I asked, "Kay, how have you survived losing Doug? Where have you gotten the strength?"

Without the slightest pause, Kay answered as though the answer was obvious, "It's what Doug would have expected of me. I couldn't do less. I didn't want to fail him or me." What a stunning answer. I caught my breath.

Kay continued, "When I lost Doug, I became an extension of him, and over the years I have tried to emulate him. He was a person who loved life and would have wanted me to keep living. He was always so proud of me. I wanted that feeling to continue. If I had fallen apart, he wouldn't have been happy. Doug didn't want his loved ones to be sorrowful."

I turned this over in my mind. Hadn't I felt the same way? When I planted flowers, when I took the Excel computer classes, hadn't I thought, "Dick, what do you think? Don't you love the new guestroom? Look how our perennials came back! Aren't you glad that I had the house painted and new gutters installed, just like we planned? Dick, are you amazed that I'm taking these computer classes on my own? Are you pleased that I am managing the finances?"

And occasionally I would say, "Dick, I'm doing okay. I'm filling my life with some good stuff. I'm even taking that Creative Writing class that you encouraged me to do for years. I really do want you to be proud of me, especially now, because now everything is harder."

Kay had articulated what I had instinctively and silently been doing, living my life in a way that would please Dick and make him proud. Kay was handing me a precious gift: We live on for the people we have lost. Our best tribute to them is to lead a good life.

The room was still, as if our minds were catching up with our hearts. From my reverie, I realized that Kay was speaking again. "Did I ever tell you about the rainbows?"

Kay's face was radiant as she began talking about the man she had admired and loved. Doug was a fisherman, hunter, skier, golfer, successful businessman, devotee of classical music and jazz, superb cook, Dad par excellence. Every day he spent time with each of his three children, playing ball, helping with home-work, traveling, taking courses together.

Kay continued, "One of Doug's favorite activities was fly-fishing. Each year for sixteen years he and his buddies took a trip to Idaho to fish for trout. The trip was scheduled that year for June. Although he was not feeling well, Doug planned to go. Then on June 2, 1983, Doug was diagnosed with a rare cancer of the blood. The doctor would not let him go on the trip. Treatment must begin. The doctors told Doug he would live 26 months. Three months later, on September 22, 1983, Doug was gone."

Pausing to touch a tear on her cheek, Kay said, "I was right there in the hospital room. I saw all the tubes and machinery, and I watched the doctors and nurses working on him. But they couldn't save him. I knew it was over, but I didn't think I could leave him. How could I just walk out of that room? Then something happened, something I can't explain. As I was standing there, unable to move, I saw his spirit leave his body. I knew that the figure lying on that bed was not Doug. Doug had left. If I hadn't seen his spirit leave, I would probably still be standing in that room. When that happened, I was able to walk out."

Kay planned a viewing and a service for all the people who had known and cared about Doug, but she decided against a traditional burial. One evening, in a flash, she knew that she would have his body cremated. The following spring his ashes would be spread at the special place he had loved so much, the Henry's Fork of the Snake River, the site of his annual fishing trips.

"I wanted Doug's next life to be effervescent, bubbling along, having fun," Kay explained.

"Do you know anything about fishing?" Kay asked me.

"Not really. Dick was a fisherman. He used to go up to Canada sometimes. But I know nothing about fishing."

Kay explained, "Fishermen use special flies to attract the fish. Trout are very particular, so the flies must match the actual bugs that hatch on the water. And it is even more complicated than that because the hatches are different at different times of the year. Doug was a perfectionist. His favorite fly was called the Blue Wing Adam, which in fact was what the fishing group called themselves: the Blue Wing Adam Gang," she smiled, recalling the excitement of the eleven men as they left on their trip every summer.

She continued, "About the flies. First Doug tied his own flies. Then he would use indelible pencils and recolor the flies so they would match the hatches. You cannot imagine what tedious, painstaking work this is. But for Doug Johnson they had to be perfect!" Kay paused a moment.

"Do you remember I told you about our lodge up North? Well, we called it the Hatchmatcher."

I grinned, "Sounds to me like it was Doug who was the Hatchmatcher!"

"You're right!" Kate agreed. "And Doug was a great fisherman. Years later, someone gave me a fishing calendar, with scenes of fishing sites from all over the country. As I flipped through, there was a picture of the Snake River, and below was a list of the best fisherman of the area. My eyes wandered down the list. And there I saw the name, 'Doug Johnson.'"

The following June, John, a member of the Gang, offered to sprinkle Doug's ashes at the men's favorite fishing site. At first Kay considered going to Idaho but decided that she didn't need to be there. And it would just be too hard. Before leaving on the trip, John came to pick up the urn. He explained to Kay that they couldn't plan exactly when they would open it.

"It will be in the evening—which one will depend on the weather. But we'll be right there at the Henry's Fork, where we always do our fish cookout. I'll call you in the evening."

That summer, Kay's daughter Linda lived with Kay in her home. One Tuesday morning, Linda called out to Kay, "Mom, I'm late for work. See ya later!" In her mind's eye Kay followed her daughter down the narrow gravel road, going west toward the main road, down a hill and across a little bridge. Suddenly Linda was back in the house, screaming with excitement. What could have brought her back in such a tear?

"Mom, Mom, I have just had the most amazing experience of my whole life! I drove through the colors of the rainbow! I was on one side, and I could see the houses on the other side of the rainbow! It was truly awesome!" Deeply moved, Kay and Linda held each other.

Several hours later John called from Idaho. "I have an amazing story to tell you, Kay. Tonight, after our day of fishing, the skies were clear and the air very still. We knew this was the perfect night for the memorial service. In his honor we prepared Doug's favorite meal, Trout Amandine. We all drank a toast to Doug. After dinner, we stood around the little drift boat at the shoreline in our waders. I sat at one end of the boat and read the eulogy and service I had written to honor our dear friend.

"We were just ready to open the urn. It was so calm, Kay, it was like being in a cathedral at sunset. There hadn't even been a faint breeze all evening. Just at that moment a tremendous wind came up and blew the ashes all over the river. Then as quickly as it came up, it stopped. We all looked up and in the sky we saw a huge, double rainbow. We were all weeping."

Kay paused, and we were silent for several long minutes. Curled up in the leather chair, I felt a shiver and then felt tears rolling down my face. We were both quietly weeping. Kay's gentle voice slid into my consciousness.

"And now you know why I love rainbows. And the rainbows that day symbolized a very spiritual connection between God and Doug and me."

"What a blessing you had," I said.

"Oh, yes. And even after 16 years, I see rainbows as a blessing. I let this be a blessing. I let things take hold rather than shutting them off from myself. I let myself be open."

It had been a long evening. "Do you ever dream about Doug?" I asked.

"Very seldom. Do you dream about Dick?"

I answered, "Not really. I wish I could. It would seem like a visit."

Just as Kay was leaving, she turned to me, smiled and said softly, "By the way, the fish that the men catch in the Henry's Fork are rainbow trout."

We hugged good night. Kay had shared her deepest thoughts and feelings with me. We had become closer in a way that touched us both very deeply.

That night I slept hard until about 6 A.M. I tossed a little then fell asleep again. And for the first time, I had a vivid dream about Dick. He was home. In the dream I said to him, "Then these last four months didn't happen! You didn't really die." Somehow the dream made me feel happy.

In the morning I awoke to a bright, sunny day. Speaking aloud, I said, "Happy Father's Day, Doug and Dick. We love you. And if you don't mind a suggestion, this would be a perfect day for you two to go fishing."

Peter the Stonecutter at work.

CHAPTER 10

The Black Stone

In the Jewish tradition, the family places a headstone at the grave within the first eleven months after a death. A special dedication service marks the official end of the mourning period.

In early June, Karen, Fred, and I went to the monument company to select a headstone for our dear brother, father, husband.

I had anticipated wandering through uncut chunks of granite. But when we entered the store, we were instantly in what can only be described as an indoor cemetery, a compressed graveyard without grass or trees. On the floor were headstones of all shapes and sizes and colors—tall, rounded, square, flat, stark, ornate, dark, light, black, red, gray—all solid reminders of man's mortality.

The headstones were engraved, and I could read many family names that I recognized. I felt as though I were reading other people's family secrets. Or did I perhaps feel some comfort in seeing familiar names?

We slowly acclimated to the discomfort we felt in this strange place. None of us had ever faced this task, and I could see that Fred and Karen were also quite shaken. Peter, the proprietor, was a pleasant man with a Russian accent. He was short and solid, with thick hands and muscular arms. He greeted us casually. For him this was business as usual. Tombstones were his stock in trade. We shook his hand and began our work.

First we looked at the samples. Several weeks before, I had gone to the cemetery to study the stones near Dick's gravesite, a macabre mission indeed. After wandering around this silent city of strange architecture, I had decided that I preferred what was called the beveled style. Mounted on a raw, unfinished block of stone was a flat, rectangular gravestone, like a tabletop, bearing the inscription. Sitting close to the ground, the back is angled up about four inches higher than the front, making it easier to read for someone walking by.

The top of the stone provides a large surface where visitors would place small stones, an ancient Jewish tradition. The stones show that the loved one has not been forgotten. These are not special stones, just ordinary, timeless pieces of the earth. The stones accumulate as each person leaves a token of his visit.

On my second visit to the cemetery, on impulse, I took a seashell to place at the gravesite. Why? Dick loved the sea and he died in the sea. I thought he would like a memento that was different and meaningful, and that perhaps, wherever Dick is, he would smile with pleasure. I knew he would understand. It felt right and it pleased me.

Karen and Fred were satisfied with the beveled style, although I had the feeling they would have chosen differently. Still, they seemed content to go along with my choice. That settled, Peter told us that the most reasonable and most popular selection *(popular?)* was the plain granite, a mottled gray stone. I had seen many at the cemetery.

"That looks fine to me," Karen said flatly.

"I like it," agreed Fred in the same tone. They looked at me.

"It's fine," I said.

Maybe we all just wanted to get out of this morbid place.

My eyes wandered around while Peter began to explain costs. Costs? A shiver moved through my body. We must now consider the comparative prices of gravestones. As we listened to the retail price list, I tried to concentrate. This would be my last—and most lasting—decision that would reflect my husband. What would best honor the man he had been?

My mind wandered. One part of Dick loved informality. I saw him in his weekend attire: worn dock shoes, cut-offs, and a vintage t-shirt. He was cleaning his scuba gear, trimming the hedges, puttering at his tool bench, hanging a yellow tennis ball from the garage rafters to guide me in parking my car.

He loved having friends over and was famous for his annual Super Bowl parties. He would pull on his green and gold Green Bay Packers sweatshirt, draw a large betting board and set it on a tripod in the den, place a TV in every room, order an eight-food sub, and heartily welcome each guest. When the game started, he would settle into his favorite spot, a black leather Eames chair, put his feet up on the ottoman and yell for his team.

That image dissolved, and I recalled the night several years ago when Dick drove home in a new car, a sleek, black sedan with black leather interior. After driving a Volvo for twelve years and 100,000+ miles, and then test-driving cars for a year, he chose a quiet, elegant car. He emerged carrying his smooth black leather brief case and wearing a dark gray pinstriped suit with a white button-down shirt and his favorite Tabasco tie. He was a happy man.

Then another scene surfaced. It was last March, and Dick was walking me down the aisle at Bruce and Jodi's wedding. I remembered how he had searched for weeks for just the right silver and gold vest to set off the black tuxedo, how he had shined the patent leather shoes, how carefully he had put on the starched white shirt and inserted the silver cufflinks. Some men look and feel silly in tuxedos. Dick, with his straight salt-and-pepper hair, his trim physique, and his bright dark brown eyes had looked comfortable, proud, and distinguished.

Blinking away tears, I was suddenly back in the shop. We were choosing Dick's gravestone. Abruptly my eyes were drawn to a stone that they missed earlier. The tabletop was a smooth, finely-polished black granite rectangle, mounted on a rustic block of nearly black granite. If a gravestone can be beautiful, this one was.

"Wait," I said, pointing to the black stone. "I like that one."

Peter told us the price, considerably more than the original choice.

"That's the one I want," I declared. I turned to Karen and Fred. "Is that okay with you?"

"It's up to you," Karen said, and Fred nodded his assent.

"Is that a good choice?" I asked Peter.

"Absolutely. The writing is much easier to read and the color won't change. It will always keep its sheen."

He told us how gray granite becomes dark and yellowish within a few years. Some people even have these stones refinished.

And so it was decided: the glossy black granite. I felt as though a heavy weight was lifted. I knew that Dick would want something unique. He would want a stone that was rich, solid, and distinctive.

We were ready to leave when Peter asked us what we wanted inscribed on the stone. What letter fonts? What sizes? More decisions. We were exhausted. We inhaled and once again turned to our task. Would we like a Star of David? Many people inscribe a series of Hebrew letters, which mean, "May his soul be bound up with God."

Some discussion ensued. Fred and Karen seemed in some doubt. For me the question was, "What would Dick want?" I knew the answer.

"I would like the star and the letters," I said.

Mindlessly, we pointed to fonts and sizes from a book.

Finally, somber but relieved, we walked out together into a blast of dry heat and the glaring sunlight of a June day in an urban shopping mall. I felt as though I had just returned from a long and arduous trip to a foreign country.

Despite the emotional toll of our morning's work, I felt happy. I knew beyond any doubt that this was the stone Dick would have wanted, the one he would have liked the best, with exactly the right inscriptions.

More than that, in my heart and in my soul, I knew that Dick had been with us in that bizarre bazaar. It was Dick who had directed me to the black stone. I knew I would never have a moment's doubt or qualm about my choice, because in truth, it had not been my choice at all.

CHAPTER 11

The Uprazer

When you approach Shari Miller's house on a beautiful mid-July day, you will note the neatly trimmed hedges and lawn. Your eyes will focus on the generous pots of fuchsia geraniums and lobelia on either side of the door. To the right are bunches of white, fuchsia, and lavender impatiens flowing out of the staggered openings in a handmade hanging clay funnel. If you wander around to the patio in the back, you'll catch your breath at the tall, blue-red menarda, the lilies, deep purple irises, and all the happy, healthy greenery.

Shari, tall and attractive, will greet you with a warm smile and probably a hug. Her blue-green eyes may explain her love of the color blue. She has softly curled brown hair and a smooth, clear complexion.

As you enter the house and look around, you sense light flooding the house. The carpet is powder blue, the walls white, the sofa and chairs cream. On the walls are splashes of bright colors: shades of pink and purple, reds, yellows, greens, and blues. Classical music plays quietly in the background. You know that this is a happy home and that the people who live here love life.

And that is how it was in this house for many years. Shari and Rex Miller literally grew up together. They began dating when Shari was 18 and Rex, 22. He was a tall, handsome man with brown eyes and classic features.

After high school graduation, Rex started college but two factors prompted him to leave school: his restlessness with studying and his desire to travel. This was the era of the Korean War. At 18, Rex joined the Air Force with dreams of flying. Much to his disappointment, he was myopic and too tall to fly; instead of becoming a pilot, he became a radar mechanic, operating radar sites in Florida and Mississippi.

After his military stint, Rex returned to his home, attended college for two years, then took several business classes and earned his real estate license. After selling real estate for several years, he went to work in the real estate department of the electric company, where he quickly learned the process of acquiring right-of-ways and easements.

Shari and Rex married in 1956 and had two children, Elizabeth and Steven. With a growing family, Rex was ready to move on in his career. When he heard of openings for trainees at an appraisal company, he took an aptitude test and scored the highest of any applicant. A job offer put the family in a quandary: the position included travel and a cut in pay.

"We decided that this was a real opportunity," explained Shari. "I remember standing at the front door weeping, with our two small children clinging to me as we all waved good-bye. Rex was leaving for three weeks in Indiana where he would learn to do highway condemnation work, which involved appraising buildings that the state needed to purchase in order to widen a highway."

Shari laughed, remembering those early years. "Somehow I made it through. Every night when the kids went to bed, I sat down at my sewing machine and sewed. "

Rex learned so well that the company sent him to the Appraisal Institute for schooling. The work was rigorous—classes, studying, exams. Finally Rex received his highly coveted appraiser designation.

In the 1970s, with over ten years' experience under his belt, Rex left the company and joined a firm owned by two other men. When one died, Rex and the other man formed a partnership. Rex appraised land and buildings, and he often served as an expert witness in court. Once he testified in a case where the parties involved discovered that the land under their homes had been a dumpsite. Another case involved unrelenting noise from a nearby factory. Rex also testified in divorce cases where the value of a home was in contention. Other cases involved tax disputes that he helped settle. He loved the variety in his work and said he never stopped learning. Modest about his accomplishments, Rex always said he was lucky to have found something he loved to do.

One of the most highly respected appraisers in the community, Rex was elected president of the state chapter of the Institute of Real Estate Appraisers. Rex loved to share what he knew. A warm, giving man, he took great pleasure in teaching and mentoring. He enjoyed bringing young people into the field and helping to teach them. For fun he taught classes in appraising for a local real estate school. The school administrator used to say, "There's nobody like Rex!"

Shari grew up in the same hometown. She and Rex married between semesters of her senior year in the School of Education. She taught for four years until shortly before Elizabeth was born. When both children were in school full-time, Shari returned to her career and worked for the next twenty-two years, retiring in 1992.

"I loved teaching, especially the challenge of working with young children and their families." Her warmth and sensitivity served her students well.

When the children were young, the Millers would often incorporate Rex's business trips with vacations. Once they all went to New Orleans and then drove through the Smoky Mountains. When the children grew up, Shari and Rex took advantage of their flexible schedules to travel on their own, visiting Spain, Morocco, England, France, Aruba, Mexico, Hawaii, and Israel.

"Our last big trip was to Italy in 1993," Shari smiled. "Let me show you something."

She led me into the living room and opened a beautiful etagere. With great care she lifted out an elegant cobalt blue decanter, hand-blown and hand-painted for the couple by a well-known non-Jewish Venetian craftsman who spoke and wrote Hebrew.

In white Hebrew letters was the blessing over the wine, a prayer offered by Jews the world over on every Shabbat: "*Baruch Atta Adonai Eloheynu Melech Ha'olam Boray P'ri Hagafen . . .*" ("Blessed art Thou, O Lord our God, who hast created the fruit of the vine.") On the bottom of the bottle the artist had printed *Shari and Rex Miller.* Shari's pleasure in the bottle and in her precious memories beamed across her face.

"Rex and I also became very interested in art, and we loved going to art auctions. At first we were a little shy, but soon we learned what we liked."

We crossed the room and stood in front of a piano. "Look at this lithograph," and she pointed to a complex image of a man's face. "Stand back," Shari said. Suddenly I recognized the face. It was Beethoven. "I call it *The Genius,*" she said. It was an apt description of this riveting piece.

We wandered back into the den. Shari's face was joyful as she recalled her life with Rex. "We always made things fun. We enjoyed theater, and we had season tickets to the symphony." Once again I was aware of the music that was playing

Shari smiled, "We also went to Las Vegas many times. Rex loved that. He had a very engaging personality. That was why he was so well liked. He had his golf group and his card group. He also loved to read. He always kept one book on the table next to his chair in the den and one on the nightstand."

Books and family pictures filled the room. A shelf contained a varied and whimsical collection of elephants. "Rex admired elephants. He found them majestic." We returned to the etagere to admire two tiny ivory elephants, one a gift from a cousin who had served in India during World War II.

"Look at this picture," said Shari, pointing to a photograph of Rex sitting on a motorcycle that belonged to his son-in-law. "Rex was quite ill by then, but for that brief moment, driving once around the circle driveway, he forgot himself." The picture revealed no sign of his physical state; here was a happy man, excited to be riding that motorcycle.

My eyes stopped on an object on the hearth, a license plate reading *UPRAZER.* Shari chuckled, "We wanted a plate that said *Appraiser* but all the usual spellings were taken, so I came up with a phonetic spelling. One day a parking attendant in the performing arts parking garage saw the plate and asked Rex, 'Say, what's an Up-raiser? Is that like a hell-raiser?'"

"You've got it!" answered Rex.

Rex's days of joyful living ended abruptly. For over a year he did not feel well. In January 1997, Shari and Rex learned that Rex had pancreatic cancer. "On the day the doctor gave us the diagnosis, we both received a death sentence. When I wept, the doctor put his arms around me. Rex told me he needed me to be strong. I stopped crying.

Still in shock, we decided to seek another opinion. After speaking with Rex's cousin, an oncologist at Sloan-Kettering, we flew to New York. Then we returned home and Rex went through exploratory surgery. The treatment prescribed was chemotherapy."

"How did you get through all those months?" I asked.

Shari answered quickly, "I had such purpose during Rex's illness. I would get up and make breakfast for him; I was with him every day. I felt that if I took excellent care of him, he would live longer. I put the inevitable at the back of my mind. He was very strong. Our children were very attentive and we all pulled together. This terrible disease made us closer. The phone rang constantly, family and friends wanting to connect. Rex knew he wouldn't survive, but he acted upbeat. He said he would fight it to the end, and he did. Rex was just so courageous through the whole ordeal."

Prior to Rex's first chemotherapy treatment, the rabbi visited and offered encouragement. As he was leaving, he said to Rex, "You're going to be fine."

"I know I'm going to be fine. I'm in good hands," smiled Rex, putting his arm affectionately around his dear friend's shoulder, "Closer to God I can't get!"

A memory that Shari cherishes occurred in late November. An attorney called upon Rex to give an important deposition. The lawyer and a legal secretary came to the house.

"Sick as he was, Rex gave that deposition. My heart was filled with pride as he sat in his easy chair, stretching himself physically and mentally to do what he loved best, to work at his profession again. He was always such a presence, even near the end. And my heart was breaking, because I knew this would be his last time. When it was over, Rex was tired, but very satisfied."

With Shari's loving care, Rex survived until late January 1998, one year after the dreaded diagnosis and one day before their forty-second anniversary. Shari had faced the inevitable, and so Rex's death was not a shock. "Rather, there was a state of disbelief that it actually came to this. It's so terrible because it makes you realize that so much of life is out of our control."

Rex had instructed Shari that he wanted a graveside service. Because of the weather, she was concerned. Fortunately the funeral took place on a rare, mild January day.

"When we arrived at the cemetery, it was as though the Red Sea had parted. People moved aside so we could drive through," said Shari softly, her voice quivering a little. "A large crowd of people had come out to honor my husband. I was overwhelmed and tears came because of this enormous tribute to Rex."

We each sipped the peach iced tea she had prepared. Then I asked quietly, "Shari, how have you survived?"

"I hold it inside. Even though I'm very outgoing, I'm a very private person. In the year and a half since Rex died, I have had tremendous support. To carry on alone, to be able to get up in the morning—everything was an effort at the beginning. At first I was exhausted, from grieving and from the months of care giving. I slept a lot. Grieving is fatiguing." I nodded in agreement.

Shari continued, "This may sound silly, but soon after Rex died, I moved from my usual spot on the couch to Rex's chair. I realized that I couldn't bear to look at it empty." I told her that I had put a teddy bear and a blanket in Dick's chair because I too couldn't face the emptiness. She understood and we both were silent for a few minutes, lost in our own grief.

Then Shari said, "You know, when a parent dies, you grieve, but it's what you expect. Your mate is your life. Still it gets easier. We get as much help as we can. We have our support groups, we talk to people. I am fortunate to have so many lovely friends and relatives, my brother and his family, Rex's cousins." We looked at some more family pictures. Happiest of all was a picture dated July 1997, from the wedding of their daughter Elizabeth and her husband Rick. Rex looked very handsome.

"And of course, my children and their spouses have been exceptional. I talk to them daily. They have helped me in so many ways. You admired my flowers— Elizabeth is my gardener. She did all of the flowers near the patio. Steven has assisted me in financial matters. I am so grateful for my children. Both couples are attentive and they include me in many of their activities. They haven't faded."

With her innate wisdom, Shari reached out when she felt the need. She called several local hospitals and joined a grief group where a nurse practitioner was the facilitator. "She was wonderful. We met the first and third Thursday of the month. Our group consisted of a few men and women, all professional people. You bond with people who are in the same boat, and you learn from them. It was the one place I could go and talk at length about my husband. We all had a lot of respect for each other. It was very helpful to meet people at different stages of grieving."

She also joined the synagogue's weekly Grief Group. "I liked the meetings at the synagogue. They offered a different perspective and strong, lasting friendships."

As time went on, Shari found herself caught up in ongoing life around her. "There were things I had to do. That summer I sold Rex's car because the children and I just couldn't bear to look at it. I'd never sold a car before, but I put an ad in the paper and sold it. I was really proud of myself—that was quite an accomplishment!" Shari also resumed other activities: volunteer work, classes, traveling and exercising.

We both needed to stretch, and we ambled back into the living room, that warm haven of light, color, and serenity. No decorator had created these walls. Together Shari and Rex had added each piece of artwork. Each had a story and significance in their lives. Proudly Shari continued to be my docent. Above the sofa was a striking piece. "This is a serigraph by Itzchak Tarkay, an Israeli artist and Holocaust survivor. It is called *Second Thought.*"

Close to the viewer was a pensive woman in a blue and gray floppy, brimmed hat and a long multicolored scarf. You could almost feel the colors and the texture. The woman seemed to be waiting and thinking. Shari picked up a hand-signed book of Tarkay's work and opened it to a facsimile of *Second Thought.* Her pride and pleasure in her artwork shone in her smiling explanations.

In the house were three works by Yaacov Agam, another famous Israeli artist. In the den was *Akeda,* an intricate, colorful serigraph of Isaac carrying the wood for his sacrifice. The couple had purchased this piece by Shrega Weil on their trip to Israel. We also admired an abstract by Vasarely called *Day into Night,* acquired at a gallery as an anniversary gift to each other.

Shari told me how she and Rex enjoyed going to art auctions—and not just as spectators. He never hesitated to join the bidding.

"How did he do it—just raise his hand? Wasn't he nervous?"

"Once we both agreed on a piece, and on our price limit, there was no stopping him! I just watched while he did the bidding."

Shari smiled, recalling those exciting times. "You know, I wasn't sure I could ever bid on my own, but a year ago I was at an auction with friends and saw another Tarkay that I admired. I raised my hand, placed my bid and bought it myself. Rex gave me the courage. It's through him that I can do all these things. And you know what? It was exciting. I told you, we made things fun." This purchase became a special gift for her son and daughter-in-law, who had admired the artist's work.

Then Shari volunteered, "Being on my own has really toughened me. It has made me stronger."

"What is the bravest thing you've done?" I asked.

Without hesitation, Shari answered, "Besides dealing with the crushing blow of Rex's illness, it was going to Turkey and Greece with my lifelong friend Joy—no question! That trip was in June of 1999, fortunately before the devastating earthquakes. Joy and I booked our trip on January 2. When fighting broke out in Kosovo, and a rebel Kurdish leader in Turkey was sentenced to death, we didn't know what to do. There were bombings in Istanbul and Athens. People were avoiding the area. We called the State Department hotline constantly for updates on the situation."

"Did you consider canceling the trip?" I asked.

"Yes. But we decided that we would only cancel if the government issued a travel warning." The fighting in Kosovo stopped three weeks before their departure date.

For a week before leaving, Shari kept asking herself, "Am I actually doing this without Rex?" She had traveled to visit friends, but leaving the country was more difficult.

"He was always there for me. That he wasn't here to experience this with me gave me so much grief. I kept thinking, 'Why can't you be here to enjoy this?' That was the eternal, agonizing, answerless question."

The trip was a good one, and the women enjoyed the sights, the cruising, the history, and the beauty. Shari had some hard moments, thinking about Rex. "I told Joy how I was feeling, but I didn't want to spoil her trip. It took some real effort at first, and then I lost myself in the experience of the trip.

"When I got home I was profoundly grieving, almost as I had a year ago. Part of this was the tiredness. Last week during the younger Kennedy's tragedy, I heard a rabbi on television speaking about grief. He said, 'It hits you out of the blue. It's always there.' He was so right."

After a few minutes of silence, I said, "Shari, I have to ask: what has given you the strength for your journey?"

She collected her thoughts. "I don't know what gave me the strength. I only know that somewhere along the way I made a definite decision that I was going to carry on the way that Rex did. I wanted to continue being good company with other people. I keep a smile on my face. No one likes to be around someone who is always moping and sad. I have my sad times when I'm alone, and that is my choice."

She paused and spoke more about Rex. "I wanted to emulate his style of handling life's problems, and you cannot imagine the effort it took at first. But I would rather people admire me than think I'm a pain in the you-know-what! This way I feel better about myself."

Then she added, as if to explain her unladylike epithet, "You must have a sense of humor. I learned that too from Rex." We laughed lightly in agreement on that. I thought how proud Rex would be of his wife.

"Is this part of your nature?" I asked.

"Probably. I am still grieving, but as long as I'm in good health, I feel very fortunate. I have come a long way in a year and a half, and I work at being optimistic. My enjoyment of life is returning."

Shari smiled, then looked at me shyly and said, "I would like to share an experience that my children and I had. In the late spring following Rex's death, I decided to plant a tree, a handsome crimson king maple, in his memory. We selected a lovely site on Rick and Elizabeth's land, a place where the tree could grow larger and stronger in the future.

"That evening we went out right before dusk. We were concerned because the sky was growing cloudy and the air was misty. Luckily, the rains did not come, and we quietly completed our task. Just as we patted the last soil around the six-foot tree, we all looked up at the sky to the east. I don't know why. Suddenly, long past the hour when such things happen, through the mist we saw a beautiful rainbow, delicate reds, blues, yellows, and greens. We were overcome with emotion. Rick voiced what we all felt, 'Rex is here with us.' I agreed. We all felt his presence. That moment gave me such comfort." Shari and I sat in silence, tears in our eyes.

A little while later, as I walked through the foyer beside the colorful, airy living room, past the fuchsia flowers, and down the curved walkway, I felt a lightness inside that I had not known in a long time. Shari and I had spent two hours talking about one of life's saddest experiences; yet, I was leaving her house feeling peaceful. Shari and Rex had shared a delight in life that was palpable inside and outside their home. It was she who was carrying on their *joie de vivre*. Now she was the *Uprazer*. This lovely woman had reawakened in me a sense of beauty and hope. She had raised up my spirits.

CHAPTER 12

Paulette's Visit

On that terrible trip home from Hawaii my new friend Paulette gave me comfort and held me when I was beyond shock, beyond grief. She gave me the connection to Dick that I needed so desperately. In the months since January, Paulette had become very dear to me. We kept in touch by phone and soon we began talking about a future visit. Much to my surprise, Paulette announced that she would drive up from Ohio in June with her friend Laura, the woman who had told me that Dick died of an aneurysm.

On June 28, 1999, Paulette and Laura arrived to spend a few days with me. I was thrilled that they both were here, in Dick's and my home, surrounded by his pictures, his memories, his spirit. I was intrigued and open to all possibilities and looked forward eagerly to seeing Paulette again. I hoped that we might be able to recapture the spiritual connections of January.

Paulette had told me about past-life regressions. I was intrigued. Recently I had read Dr. Brian Weiss' book *Many Lives, Many Masters* [2], a highly credible book about a woman in therapy who visited her past lives. Paulette asked if I would like to try such a journey, just to see what might happen. I decided that this would require only a minor leap of faith. It could be interesting, and it would help prepare me for the session I most anticipated, when Paulette would speak with Dick.

Our first session occurred on a bright summer day. We sat in the den, Paulette in Dick's recliner, Laura and I opposite her. The house was completely still. The session lasted about two hours. Because the pace was slow, I was able to take notes.

Following are excerpts from my transcripts of that session. Bracketed, italicized text is to clarify information or describe my feelings at the time.

A JOURNEY BACK IN TIME: A PAST-LIFE REGRESSION
Morning, June 29, 1999

Paulette: Make up a story about yourself and Margie in another time and place. *[I later learned this was a technique to take me to a relaxed, altered state of mind.]*

Diane: We're in medieval times. Margie is a princess, wearing a long white dress and gold shoes. I am a lady-in-waiting, her companion. We are young girls, and we mischievously sneak into the Queen's room and try on her bracelets, just for fun.

We are going on a picnic. The Queen visits us for a while; then she leaves. The princess has a small, curly-haired puppy. Gradually he is transformed and becomes a prince. He reaches out for Margie's hand, turns to me and asks, "Is it okay now?"

They hold each other, and I fade into the background.

Paulette: Now I want you to walk down a path, away from them. Go to another time. You can go farther into the past, or you can move into the future.

Diane: I walk down a grassy path. Soon it becomes rocky, gravelly, as I move into a dark forest.

Paulette: Now you come to a fork in the road. What do you see there?

Diane: I see a silvery fish.

Paulette: Choose one of the pathways, right or left. Which one?

Diane: To the right. *[I began to feel very relaxed, almost drowsy. Was it Paulette's soothing voice?]* I am in a hut in a forest. It looks like the Black Forest, maybe in Germany. I'm 35 now. I have two siblings, two brothers.

Paulette: Who are they?

Diane: They are my Dad and Dick. We are all about the same age.

Paulette: Is there a house?

Diane: Yes, it's very dark, rough-hewn. We have to hunt for food. It's a hardscrabble life.

Paulette: What kind of shoes are you wearing?

Diane: Not really shoes. More like suede foot coverings. And I'm wearing a rough goldish bracelet. It has been passed down through the family. I have some red, green, and gold scarves that I use for color and for fun.

[We sat in silence for a minute or two.]

Paulette: Let's move along on the journey.

[More silence.]

Diane: We are in an ancient country—Rome or Greece—no, it's Greece. I am 15 years old, and I live in a prosperous family. I have a twin brother.

Paulette: Do you recognize him?

Diane: *[I was surprised.]* It's Dick. He is my twin brother. We are very close. Our mother is tall with red hair. She is very gracious but rather aloof.

Paulette: What about your father? Do you recognize him?

Diane: He is a very dark man, but I don't recognize him. I have a special friend and playmate.

Paulette: Who is that?

Diane: It's Paulette. She has a warm, sunny disposition and we have a lot of fun.

Paulette: Move ahead five years now. What is happening in your life?

Diane: I am married to a man with dark, curly hair. I have a son and daughter. I am happy. Then my husband tells me there is another woman, but he wants to keep our marriage.

[More minutes of silence.]

Paulette: Continue your journey.

Diane*: [By now I was totally relaxed, the cat was curled in my lap, and the words poured out from somewhere deep inside me, unfettered, not created by me.]* I'm a 7- or 8-year-old boy. We live on a barren plain in Asia. I am hunting with my Dad.

Paulette: Do you recognize your Dad?

Diane: It's Dick. He is giving me very precise training about the bow and arrow and how to hunt for wild boar.

Paulette: Do you see anyone else?

Diane: I have two little sisters. They have black hair and eyes and are very mischievous.

Paulette: Move ahead a few years now.

Diane: I am a boy of 17. Now we live in a little town. My father is dead; mother is a seamstress. We have a hard time. I sweep the town square to make money. I see an adorable little blond girl with blue eyes. She looks like Margie.

Paulette: Move ahead a few years again.

Diane: I marry and live in a tent. My wife has dark eyes. She is mean to me, often rails at me.

Paulette: Look ahead again.

Diane: Now I am 40 years old. I'm living alone in the same tent. I am growing old, but I am very important in the community, almost like a shaman. People come to me for advice, for wisdom. I see a community of people struggling to exist. I am the patriarch.

Paulette: Move ahead.

Diane: I see myself passing over. It is very peaceful. Many people are mourning for me.

Paulette: Is there a lesson from this life?

Diane: Sometimes life is rough. We go through many trials. Sometimes our personal life seems empty but we make a contribution to others' lives.

Paulette: Now let's move forward in time.

Diane: It's the early 1900s. I'm a lady journalist, aged 40. I see bright lights in a room where I am at a typewriter. I like to write poetry but it isn't very good.

I have a rather solitary life. I think my friend Donna was my mother and best friend, and my Aunt Bea appeared also. I don't know what she was. I have a box of "treasures" from my family.

Paulette: Open the box. What is inside?

Diane: I see colored bead necklaces, old eyeglasses, and at the bottom in a corner I see a diamond ring. It's my wedding ring that I lost.

Paulette: Let's move forward again.

Diane: It's in the early 1940s. It's my birthday. My mother and I are wearing matching pinafore dresses.

Paulette: Let's look into the future now.

Diane: I see light, much light. But it's misty. I see a book, travel.

Paulette: Who is there?

Diane: Many, many people. I see their eyes, loving and compassionate. They are all there, just a thought away.

* * *

What do I make of this experience? I only know that somewhere after the medieval visit, I was not creating but reporting. I feel somehow connected with the scene in the Black Forest and with the journalist. However, my strongest connection is with the shaman. I have always been interested in health—I ate yogurt and healthy breads when they were only available by mail order. Maybe I was a shaman. That wouldn't be such a bad thing. Paulette and Laura were not the least bit surprised that I was a shaman.

We were finished. The journey was arduous, and I was tired, sad, and happy.

A FRISKY VISIT FROM DICK
Evening, June 29, 1999

We took our now customary seats. When we began, some light still entered the windows. We sat for about an hour. The session began with Paulette laughing heartily. What could be so amusing?

Paulette: This is so odd. I probably shouldn't even say this but I know you well enough. I hear Dick saying, "Glub, Glub, Glub!" and see him rising above the water.

[At that, I began to shake. Whenever anyone asked Dick about scuba diving, he would hold his nose with one hand, raise the other as though about to submerge, and say, "Glub, glub, glub." After hearing this at least fifty times, I thought it was silly and always predictable. I had never mentioned this to Paulette. When she quoted this phrase to me, my heart stopped and I began to cry softly. When I explained my reaction, she said, "I think he is trying to tell us that he is letting go of how he died." We sat in silence for a while; then she continued.]

Dick wants you to go see dolphins in their natural habitat. I see a very blue sea. I see you sitting beside a tank or on a boat, reaching down and stroking a dolphin.

I see you asleep. I see Dick touching your face. He's lying next to you, on your left, his left arm over you.

I see two holy men following him.

He says to you, "See it all, kid! I'm all over the place!"

I see you sitting in front of a huge computer screen, with his big smile there. He is proud of you. Sometimes he wants so much to tell you how to do it. He wants to help you on the computer.

The investments, the finances: he pats you on the back. "You've learned well."

Today he is being impish, playful. Dick, you are too much!

I sense some wistfulness about big houses. There are other priorities. He has down-to-earth concerns about insuring your future. He's saying, "After all, I did leave you the car, didn't I?"

Tonight he is very playful, immodest, very affectionate. He's happy Laura and I are here because we can hear him. He says it would be nice if you would do this for yourself again so he could talk to you. He says it's so easy. You need to have confidence you can do it.

He says, "The house looks great, kid!" He will take kitty cat with him soon. Something about tennis. He wants to go to a tennis match.

Diane: Can you learn anything about my wedding ring? *(No answer.)*

Paulette: I see a red and white boat, a replica of a ship. He's ready for more fun. He wants you to be having fun. He really wants you to be happy. He thinks you're sexy when you smile. He's cozying up to you. He's frisky!

He says, "Don't forget to show them . . ." He doesn't finish this. He says, "Goodnight."

He's a little dickens!

MY HEART IS BREAKING
Evening, June 30, 1999

This was the last, the most difficult, and the most moving session. I began taking notes but had to stop because I was crying so hard. How I wish we had taped this. The silences between questions and responses were long.

Diane: Please ask Dick about his dying.
[A long silence.]
Paulette: He's pointing down, below his heart, toward his solar plexus, an artery below his heart. He blew an aneurysm on his left side. His body was more worn out than anyone knew. He felt a twinge across his mid-section, then pins and needles spread across his stomach. That was the only sensation. He had no fear. It

was a very, very fast ascension in the light. He didn't witness the ambulance or the hospital; there was no hovering.

He is a quick learner, getting permission to be with you.

Diane: Did he send you to be with me?

Paulette: No, it was my guides nudging me to be where you were.

(To Dick) What do you want her to know? *[Here Paulette spoke Dick's words in her voice.]*

"I love you." Pause. "We're going to Jerusalem. Take me to my favorite place. An altar, a stage-like place."

Diane: I know the place, the Hurva Synagogue in the Old City. He stood where he wasn't allowed, and some lady scolded him.

Paulette: Revisit that place. He will be by your side. There is a spiritual oneness between you. He is studying with the holy men. He is moving up.

"My mother sends you a message of thanks for being good to her son."

Diane: Where is my Dad?

Paulette: He is with your Mom, near Dick but not with him.

I get confirmation that I am to take you to a waterfall. You were together quite some time ago, when you were brother and sister. He remembers the Bavarian forest as though it was yesterday, as you played gleefully, caring for one another, hiding, delighting in the forest. Dick says, *"Times were hard but we had each other, didn't we?"*

And so you walk together up a hill, look into each other's eyes, again one in mind and spirit. It's okay being brother and sister at this time. He says, "I am for you, you for me."

Now I will speak for Dick, in his words.

"There is a secret place of cleansing hearts and souls. Come walk with me, my beloved, one more time, innocent with innocent. We will walk to the waterfall, gazing eye to eye, heart to heart, soul to soul. Pledge once more the bond we share, to return again as man and woman. Together we will be once more as one.

"See it all, experience it all for me. I wish I could have told you all that I felt. I'll be with you always in spirit. Would that I could have said these words when last I stood beside you. I never meant you not to know what was in my heart. We will be one again together. Time is but a blink of the eye."

[There followed here a long and beautiful poem, about Dick and me, about love, about time. But I was crying too much to keep writing, and so the words are lost forever. I only remember that he spoke of our forever love, of being together again. When the poem was over, Dick's humor resurfaced.]

Paulette: He says he'll be the tall one next time!

That was the end of the session. How I wish I had written or recorded all those words, but I must hold onto the love and the concepts. It was Dick at his best, his most romantic, but somehow elevated in language. It was not Paulette's style, thoughts, or words.

We all went to bed, emotionally and psychically drained.

CHIMES AND A SMILEY FACE

That night I awoke at 4:15 A.M. Suddenly as I lay there, I heard the doorbell chimes.

After Dick died, I had an alarm system installed in the house. Every night when I arm the system, a red light goes on. If anyone should attempt to enter any entrance, door or window, every siren and horn would blast. When the system is disarmed, any entrance or exit prompts a 4–5 note chime. This way if I am in the back of the house, I will know if someone enters.

That night I armed the house as usual. At 4:15 I heard the chimes. How could that be? I checked the red light in my bedroom. Impossible. I must have been asleep and dreamed the sound.

Now I was awake, alert, and unable to fall back to sleep. At about 4:30 I heard the chimes again. This time I was sure. I rose and walked around the house. Everything was fine. Puzzled but sleepy, I returned to bed.

The next morning I asked Paulette and Laura if they had heard the chimes. Yes, they both had heard the chimes but thought nothing of it. They looked at each other and smiled. To them it was clear: Dick caused the chimes to ring because he wanted us all to know that he was here. He chose a night when I was not alone because otherwise I would have been frightened.

I later read in *Talking to Heaven* by James Van Praagh [3], a book about communicating with deceased people, that the easiest way for spirits to effect our plane is through electrical devices because the frequency or energy is so high. Am I crazy? I think I believe. I certainly have no better explanation for the chimes. And that makes me happy.

Months later I had occasion to speak with the alarm company. I asked if it is possible for the chimes to ring when the system is armed.

"Absolutely not. There is no way that can happen."

JULY 3, 1999

A few nights later, as I was writing about Paulette's visit and the chimes, I typed along very quickly. This entire story was spilling out. I was at the bottom of the last page, glanced up and caught the line that says, "Now I will speak for Dick, in his words . . ." ☺

At the end of the line appeared an unfamiliar symbol. I squinted, trying to see what it was. And there was a tiny smiley face, the same one Dick often drew near his name when he left little notes for me. I have never used a smiley face and have no idea how to construct on the computer.

I blinked, stared, and began shaking, crying, and hyperventilating. I ran around the room, calling Dick's name. When I pulled myself together, laughing and crying simultaneously, I was so happy to have this sign, this wonderful and amazing gift.

Calming down a bit, I said to myself, "You're just seeing things!" I would do a reality check. I would PRINT out that page. Would the smiley face show up? I doubted it. But it did. Who would believe this?

That evening I called Paulette. She was delighted, said this truly was a gift, and that it was confirmation that those were indeed Dick's words that we had heard. She told me this is not the last message I will receive from the computer.

I mulled over the elements of this event for many days: Dick's familiar symbol appearing on his computer screen and its placement on the page, in a line quoting his words.

Was it uncanny, or was it the most natural thing in the world?

I would never have the answer. What I did know was that one smiley face on a screen had taken me from startled to amazed, amused, and comforted. On that warm July day, I felt connected to my husband in a very special—and almost tangible—way.

DECEMBER 5, 2000

Many months passed and with no voices or visitors, no mysterious happenings. Early in December, I called Paulette for our quarterly catch-up chat. When I asked about Dick, she told me he is "moving on."

Yesterday I visited some old and dear friends. As we reminisced, I cried a little. Had it been two years, two weeks, or maybe a hundred years since Dick left us? My concept of time was still muddled.

For months I had been cleaning closets, files, drawers. Early in the morning of December 5, dressed in my sweats and energized by a good workout, I marched directly into the office to attack the storage closet. I didn't turn on the computer. E-mail could wait. I opened the closet doors and pulled out some empty plastic crates. Next I retrieved Dick's raggedy briefcase and his 1998 date book that I had held onto. "Time to go," I sighed.

At that moment, from the direction of the computer, came four distinct musical tones, almost like the first four notes of a melody, vaguely familiar. I looked up from my work and toward the computer. There it sat, silent, stoic. Had I turned it on and forgotten? No.

Odd. I paused, absently wondering where the sounds had come from. I was alone in the house; I have no musical instruments. No TV or CD player was on. The wind chimes were outside and far from the office. I turned back to the closet and finished my project.

An hour later I turned on the computer. When the Windows screen appeared, I heard four musical notes—the same ones I had heard earlier. Suddenly I remembered the smiley face, the chimes, and the theory that spirits can most easily make their presence known through electronics. A shiver ran through me.

Later in the morning I called our friend Howard and asked, "Have you been thinking about Dick lately?"

Oh, yes, he was aware of the upcoming anniversary. Dick was much on his mind. He had even bought a *yahrzeit* candle and was preparing a little memorial service. How dear. Dick would have been pleased that his dearest friend was thinking of him.

"Howard, I want to tell you what happened today." When I finished the story, I said, "It makes me think that maybe Dick was here."

"Not maybe," responded Howard. "He was there."

With humor I could not have mustered 18 months ago, I joked, "Well, it sure would be nice if he would come help me do all this cleaning!" We both laughed.

That afternoon a light, flaky snow drifted past my office window. It wasn't officially winter yet, but it was as cold, dreary, and still as any January day. My eyes filled. Dick, was that you, here to say, "Hi, how are you?"

I liked hearing the notes. I felt peaceful all day long.

CHAPTER 13

To Catch the Fog

When you meet Ramona Rogers you will place her into a 17th century Velasquez painting as an aristocrat of Spanish royalty. Standing only 5'2", she is slim, petite, and softly feminine. Her heart-shaped face hosts smooth olive skin, straight white teeth, dark brown almond-shaped eyes, long dark hair cut in a neat bob, high cheekbones, and tiny dimples that appear when she laughs. For the painting you will dress her in a dark velvet dress and white lace mantilla. She will gaze out at you mysteriously from behind a fan, no doubt ready to whisper of some intrigue in her life.

Ramona does not wear a mantilla. Instead, she is beautifully groomed in classically stylish clothes. She prefers sportswear. For a casual lunch she may wear a pair of perfectly tailored camel hair slacks with a matching cashmere sweater and cape, which she wears with flair. Who but Ramona could carry this off? On her, the cape is as right as the mantilla in the painting.

When Ramona speaks, she has a slight accent, with captivating r's rolling around like playful fish in a pool. Her voice is low and measured; no word is wasted. Her demeanor has a quiet dignity and elegance. Captivated, you listen attentively to every word and idea.

Born Ramona Vasquez in Sabinas, Mexico on December 7, 1947, she is the oldest of ten siblings. Her mother is Mexican, and her father is a native Texan. She describes her family as "non-religious Catholics." At 15 Ramona left home and went to a private boarding high school. After high school Ramona attended a teachers college for a year, until she decided that teaching elementary school was not what she wanted to do. She became interested in bilingual education, which required that she become proficient in English. She enrolled in a one-year total-immersion language institute in Monterey, Mexico, to improve her English. From there she went to a private women's college, where she received a degree in bilingual business administration.

Ramona's parents were merchants in Mexico. When Ramona was 20, the family immigrated to Chicago for a business opportunity. Because her father was an American citizen, Ramona's visa came quickly, with no waiting period. Once in Chicago, Ramona enrolled at the Circle Campus of the University of Illinois in a one-year program for foreign students. Her goal was to perfect her English.

After graduation she took a job as an assistant manager in a real estate office in a Hispanic neighborhood. Always inclined toward the arts, Ramona signed up for night classes in art, music, and decorating. For three years she also studied dress design, another lifelong interest. (Aha, so that's where she learned how to put herself together so beautifully!)

Samuel Rogers owned a national chain of luggage stores. In 1979 Ramona was planning a trip to Europe and needed luggage. Near her office was one of Samuel's stores, where she went shopping on her lunch hour. When she returned at 6 P.M. to pick up her new suitcase, the store was closed. As it happened, Samuel was in town, meeting with his managers. He answered the door and they met.

By now Ramona worked at Carl Fischer, a music publishing company, and was dating a baritone opera singer she had met through work. Samuel, who had been married before to a woman from the Bahamas, was seeing a French woman.

Samuel gave Ramona his business card. He had traveled all over the world, and so he suggested they get together after her trip. Later they were formally introduced. So much for the Mademoiselle and the baritone!

In March of 1981 Samuel and Ramona married. At first they lived in Chicago, commuting on weekends to Milwaukee where Sam owned a house. Eventually the couple decided to move to Milwaukee and purchased a wonderful old home.

Although Ramona was 32 to Sam's 52, she had a hard time keeping up with him. "My life took a turn when I married Samuel. He became the most important thing in my life." Because of the couple's broad interests and high energy levels, being Samuel's wife was a full-time job.

Ramona smiled as she recalled Sam's great love of travel—and his spontaneity. "One evening at dinner he asked casually, 'Oh, by the way, would you like to go to Europe in two weeks?' At first I objected, 'Samuel, I can't possibly be ready that fast!' He just laughed, 'Of course you can.' And I was. We never went on tours. All we knew when we left was generally what countries we would visit. It was so informal and so wonderful."

Ramona described Samuel as a Renaissance man, whose scope of interests included philosophy, astronomy, cooking, religions, geography, medicine, antiques, and music. His knowledge in these areas was never superficial because a field of interest for him became a field of intensive study.

Ramona was always fond of classical music, particularly Beethoven and Mozart. Samuel was a devotee of Bach and Vivaldi, and he shared his enthusiasm and knowledge with his wife. Before a trip to Italy, he told Ramona about

Vivaldi's life. A priest and teacher by profession, Vivaldi worked in an orphanage where his job was to groom young girls to marry into fine families.

One day Ramona and Sam were walking down a street in Venice, admiring the buildings and scenery, when he suddenly stopped short and planted himself firmly in front of Ramona. "When he rotated, I had to rotate as well. We were facing a building. My eyes wandered around and stopped on a bronze plaque. I read it. I shrieked, 'Oh, my God! I don't believe it!'"

When Sam asked what was wrong, Ramona screamed with delight, "This building was Vivaldi's orphanage!"

Then Sam asked, "Why do you think I stopped?"

Ramona's eyes filled. "He wanted me to have the joy of discovery myself . . . and I did!"

After her marriage Ramona's love of study and learning continued. "I consider myself a perennial student." Soon Ramona became involved in volunteer work. A businesswoman by training, Ramona also assumed the household financial matters.

A gregarious man, Sam liked to entertain friends at their twenty-foot long banquet table. "If two weeks went by without our having guests over, Samuel would complain, 'We haven't had anyone here in ages.' And we'd begin planning another dinner party." By this time Ramona was a gourmet cook and took great pleasure in entertaining at home.

The grounds of Ramona's home are a stunning mix of greenery and bright colors. She does all the gardening herself, planning, planting, and tending her magnificent flowers, which "I wouldn't trust to anyone!" She has always been involved in home projects, like decorating and collecting prized art and antiques. She has never stopped sewing. Several of the decorative pieces in her home are of her own design and creation.

By the time Ramona described all of these interests and activities, I wondered if there was anything this 100-pound dynamo could not do? Little did I know what was coming next. Ramona was on to her next accomplishment.

"Sam always wanted to have fun," Ramona beamed. "He really got a kick from flying his 172 Cessna 4-seater plane. I was so jealous of all that fun that I began to learn navigation with maps. Then I took flying lessons. With all my activities, I made time to fly twice a week. And of course I studied a lot. Finally I got my pilot's license, and I did a lot of flying."

On a cruise to South America, Samuel and Ramona had a free day in Patagonia. Instead of going on a pre-arranged tour, they inquired about an airplane. Yes, in the town of Ushuaia, they could rent a plane. They took a cab to the remote frontier town. Because of the unfamiliar territory, they hired a pilot.

"We were the only passengers on that cruise who saw the spectacular scenery of Patagonia not only from the sea but also from the air!"

While in his 40s Samuel developed Crohn's disease, a chronic condition that causes painful bowel obstructions. Samuel controlled his illness through medication for many years, under the care of a gastrointestinal specialist who happened to be a good friend of his.

In early 1993 an epidemic of cryptosporidium struck the city of Milwaukee. At first no one knew what was happening, why so many people were getting sick. Later it became clear that parasites in the drinking water were causing severe illness and even death.

"Crypto" means "secret or hidden." With cryptosporidium the parasites hide in the walls of the intestines and are extremely difficult to test for. In April 1993 Samuel became extremely ill, exhibiting the symptoms typical of Crohn's. For several weeks he was in and out of a local hospital with debilitating bouts of diarrhea. The doctors were certain this was his old illness flaring up.

Sam knew that these episodes were entirely different, but no one listened to him. "I have that parasite in my body," he told the staff. The hospital sent him home again; twenty-four hours later he was back, still suffering. Finally, in disgust and frustration, he checked himself out of the hospital and went home, very despondent. Finally Ramona called the internist. He ordered Sam to check into his hospital immediately.

"We'll keep you here, run tests, whatever is necessary. I think you're right: this isn't Crohn's. I agree with you—it may be crypto." Within a few days, Sam tested positive for cryptosporidium.

The doctor explained that the many years of Crohn's had severely compromised Samuel's immune system. By the time of the correct diagnosis, much damage had already occurred. Although his kidneys still functioned, renal failure was the new concern.

A short time later Samuel underwent surgery to place a shunt on his arm to prepare him for dialysis. This was none too soon. Within a few days, Samuel began visiting the hospital three times a week, where he was hooked up to a machine that cleansed his blood of toxins and kept him alive.

Ramona became tearful as she discussed this period of their lives. "Samuel was a free spirit. This time was very difficult for us. We had no more spontaneity in our lives. We stopped going abroad. We had to find out locations of dialysis centers wherever we went. It hurt me when he'd say, 'This is like reporting to a parole officer.'"

The earliest appointment for dialysis was at 6 A.M. Not wanting the treatments to rule his life, Samuel was at the hospital early. By 9:30 he had stopped at his favorite store to pick up fresh fruit and rolls for breakfast with Ramona. Once he told her proudly, "Most people come out of dialysis in wheelchairs. I'm walking out!"

These procedures began early in 1994 and continued for three years, two or three times a week. "It was a horrible thing for him. He referred often to 'shackles,' 'tethers,' and his parole officer. It became a kind of black humor for him. It was difficult for us both—I felt what he was going through. The emotional part was the most difficult. I wanted to do for him. I felt such helplessness."

Samuel was determined that their lives should be as normal as possible, so the couple decided to buy a condo in Matzalan, Mexico, as a getaway. When they confirmed that a dialysis clinic was opening in town, they proceeded with the purchase. The clinic never opened; the nearest dialysis unit was in the state capital three hours away. What was the choice? Samuel and Ramona took trips twice a week by bus to the city.

For the Rogers, adventures just happened.

After several arduous bus trips, the couple decided to buy a car to make the dialysis runs more convenient. On their first trip, they set out at 5 A.M. About half way there, Samuel suddenly exclaimed, "Oh my goodness—we're nearly out of gas! I was sure there would be gas stations along the way. I'm afraid we're not going to make it!"

Then they spotted a sign for a town. They started down the unpaved road and finally found the tiny town and a grocery store. Where could they buy gasoline?

"No gas station," said the lady proprietor.

They learned that one local farmer kept a small tank of gas that he sold to other farmers for their tractors. Several more unpaved back roads led to the farmhouse, where an old man interrogated them. Finally he agreed to sell some gas. When he tried to open the tank, the gas cap wouldn't budge. Samuel tried too, unsuccessfully.

"You need a strong man," said the farmer, and directed them to his friend Gavino, in a nearby house.

Ramona walked over to the house, shouting, "Gavino, Gavino!" Out came a tall, tan, very handsome man, with bare chest and dripping wet hair, fresh from the shower. He had hazel eyes and a piercing look. Ramona was taken aback. Here was this god, in the middle of nowhere! When she asked him to help, he extended his hand in greeting. Gavino was able to open the tank, the gas was delivered, and Samuel arrived on time for dialysis.

Gavino turned out to be the local veterinarian who cared for cattle in the area. He and the Rogers became friends and visited on future trips. Once on the way to Mexico, Samuel and Ramona befriended two priests from Iowa, whom they invited to visit in Mazatlan. On the next dialysis trip, the priests came along and were delighted to meet with Gavino and practice their Spanish.

From the start of his illness Ramona urged Samuel to go on a waiting list for a kidney transplant. At first Samuel was not eager for this because he would be on medications for the rest of his life, drugs with negative side effects. Two years later Ramona was watching a television program. An Hispanic woman gave a kidney to her Caucasian fiancé, who did very well. Might Ramona's kidney be compatible with Samuel's body? When she first mentioned her idea, his reaction was, "You'll never match."

Most people are born with two kidneys, which developed through evolution because early man was often injured in that area of his body. One kidney is enough to do the job, and it is possible that in future generations the second one may simply shrivel and disappear. "I'm highly evolved," Ramona joked.

Eventually Samuel became enthusiastic about the idea of a transplant. Another long course awaited them: first the extensive testing to determine compatibility, next several months of preparations. At that time Ramona donated blood every eight weeks, which was transfused to her husband so that his system would become accustomed to her blood.

Over the ten months between the decision and the surgery, Samuel kept asking, "Are you sure you want to do this? There will be a lot of pain and a lot of risk."

Sam tried to dissuade Ramona, but she was determined to give her husband every chance for a normal life, despite the fact that the doctor was skeptical. "He was concerned that Sam may not survive the surgery," Ramona explained. "Sometimes I would ask myself if I was doing this to make me feel better. Was I doing this for me or for him? I couldn't bear to see him suffer. And I knew that without the transplant, I would watch him die slowly with every dialysis."

By fall of 1996 Sam's kidneys had deteriorated further. A transplant seemed the best option. The doctors told the couple that Sam had "a 95 percent chance of success." On September 15 Sam purchased a very special bottle of champagne so that he and Ramona could celebrate his homecoming. On September 16 Samuel and Ramona shared an operating room, and the surgery was performed. Four hours later, Sam was up and around. He strolled into Ramona's room, proudly waving the urine bag. He was elated. Finally something was going right. "Look, baby," he announced to his sedated donor, "It's working!"

For the first three days, Sam's recovery was very good. He would remain in the hospital for three weeks for monitoring. The doctors released Ramona a week after the surgery. "I was weak and still in pain, but mainly I was going crazy. I wanted to go home but I didn't want to leave him. I left in tears. I felt a sense of doom. I was very, very sad. You might say I had a premonition.

"I asked Samuel, 'Should I go home?' His answer was a strange one for Samuel, who always encouraged me to progress. He said, 'It's up to you.'"

Still very weak from her surgery and heavily medicated for pain, Ramona went home on a Thursday. She rested at home one day and visited Samuel on Saturday.

On Sunday, Ramona's family came to visit. She called Samuel at the hospital. "My parents are here and they want to come visit you."

"Please tell them I love them, but I'm not up to seeing people," said Samuel. "You stay with them and come tomorrow."

It was unlike Samuel to reject company in the hospital. Ramona knew something was going on, but was distracted with family and didn't have much time to think about it. They spoke on the phone on Sunday night. On Monday, when Ramona went to the hospital, Samuel was intubated and unable to speak.

Samuel never rallied after that. Twice his body tried to reject the new kidney. Then he received anti-rejection drugs, which in turn destroyed his immune system. An infection of unknown origin developed. It would take 72 hours to analyze the culture. In the meantime he began taking wide-spectrum antibiotics. By the time the culture came back, it was too late. The infection was rampant.

Despite his terrible infection, Samuel underwent two more surgeries, one to close a wound from his original surgery that had opened and was bleeding and a second to remove his spleen, which was depleting his white blood cells. After the second surgery, Samuel never regained consciousness. To this day Ramona is sure that he knew she was there.

His body could take no more. Samuel Rogers died in early October.

*   *   *

For ten months after Samuel's death, Ramona withdrew from the world. The layers of her grief were like slabs of geological strata in the earth. The heaviest stone was her feeling of guilt. She battered herself repeatedly. When Samuel died, Ramona was still recovering from her own major surgery. Her body was in shock and in pain, a constant, palpable reminder of her final gift to Samuel.

But had it been the gift of life or the gift of death? Had Samuel died because of her kidney? Would he have lived longer without it? Had God punished her? Ramona reasoned, "Who am I to say, 'I'll give him his freedom, remove his shackles'? How arrogant of me to think that I had the key!"

Day after day, month after month she lived and relived the decision and the aftermath. Finally, through her own deep soul-searching, she knew that she had had no other choice. The weight lifted.

"Today I feel it was the right thing. As a wife, the way I loved him, I could not stand by and not do anything."

I looked at my friend in awe. How had Ramona, this small, gentle soul, slogged her way back up from under the weight of her grief?

Ramona spoke of her writing. In the days and months after Samuel's death, Ramona received hundreds of notes and letters. Many she answered herself, often composing long letters on her old-fashioned typewriter.

"Writing those letters was a kind of therapy for me," Ramona explained. "I would talk about Samuel, and I would recount the story of our life together and the kind of person I was married to. Three months later, I was still writing letters. That helped me very much."

Friends would visit but Ramona was comfortable only in her own house. "I became a kind of recluse." It was three months before she went out for dinner. On a Saturday night in January, Ramona drove out to have dinner with her brother-in-law and his wife. Leaving their home at 9:30 P.M., Ramona began the long, empty ride home.

"With no warning, I began to feel terribly sad, returning home by myself, thinking of all the times Samuel and I had taken this drive together after other lovely evenings. My tears poured out. I drove the car mechanically, not conscious that I was far exceeding the speed limit. There were no other cars on the road. Suddenly in the mirror I saw a flashing light. I changed lanes so the policeman could go by me. Then I realized that it was me he was after. That was an expensive ticket, and I didn't even have the energy to explain." Ramona's eyes filled as she remembered that terrible night. "The experience was devastating. It was a long time before I was ready to go out again. It was just too painful."

In those early months Ramona found it difficult to be around people who knew her, and she avoided any contact. When she needed to go grocery shopping, she would go at night to another part of town, to a store where she wouldn't see anyone she knew.

Her large, brown eyes were exquisitely sad as she continued, "I just was not ready for, 'I'm sorry, Ramona.' I didn't want to hear it. Gradually I was able to accept this. Now when I say 'I'm sorry,' it really means something. Nobody knows until they go through it. People are limited by their inexperience, and they distance themselves from that event. In a way, they hope that your loss and your grief have immunized them."

Ramona told a curious story that evoked strong feelings for her. Long before Samuel's illnesses, Ramona met a couple at a Thanksgiving dinner. Shortly thereafter the husband died suddenly. A year later Ramona learned that the woman had met a man and was dating. Ramona's reaction was, "It was good for her to find someone."

A mutual friend said, "Well, it didn't take her long." Ramona never forgot that comment, and she is acutely sensitive to the expectations and judgments of outsiders.

We discussed this sudden loss of privacy and the judgments. Why do people feel they have the right to judge a grieving person? Is there a schedule of acceptable activities for us? Who sets the rules?

Like so much involved in this sad process, decisions are individual. Ramona and I agreed that we all do what feels right for us, and we do it when it feels right. No pre-set timetable can dictate our feelings or actions. What feels appropriate and comfortable for one person at two weeks, a month, six months, or two years may feel all wrong for someone else. But no one has the right to pass judgment about the path of another.

When a couple is married, others generally keep a discreet distance and respect their privacy. When the couple is no longer, the shield drops and distant friends begin to ask personal questions, offer unsolicited advice, monitor activities, and censure, with a raised eyebrow or damning comment. The single woman may become fair game for gossip under the guise of quiet concern. For people who guard their privacy, this concern can seem like an invasion, at a very sensitive time. Perhaps we overreact when we feel we are suddenly living in a fishbowl. Now Ramona says that she is inured, and others have learned to respect her privacy as they did before.

I asked Ramona if she has changed.

"I don't think I have changed. I was always very strong and independent, maybe because I went away to school so young and was so completely dependent on myself. I always had the freedom to do what I wanted to do because Samuel encouraged that in me."

Then she spoke of a change she did see in herself.

"When we go through the loss, we become more sensitive to others grieving the loss of a spouse. When a husband or wife who has not lived through this says, 'I'm sorry,' they cannot begin to feel what I do. They didn't eat with this person, sleep with this person, play or rejoice with this person. They cannot imagine. I think I am more aware, more sensitive, more understanding of what other survivors are going through. Samuel's death also gave me additional strength that helped sustain my sister's death."

Ramona's youngest sister Tess was 31 when she died suddenly in the spring of 1999, just three years after Samuel's death. Samuel and Ramona had always been close with Tess. "Samuel loved Tess. We called her Little Tessie, even after she told me she wanted to be just Tess. When she died, I was devastated, shocked—this was my baby sister.

"A day or two after she died, I spoke aloud to Samuel, right here in the living room. I said, 'You probably know what I'm going to tell you—we lost our Little Tessie.' The next day I saw a mutual friend, a man who had known Tess and was aware of how much she meant to Samuel and me. He looked at me with still, serious eyes and said, 'Samuel is not alone any more. He has Tessie.'"

Ramona gasped and replied, "You're right. I never thought about it that way." For Ramona this experience was incredibly comforting, a moment and an insight that gave her deep solace.

Slowly, slowly Ramona began to return to her life, or perhaps to construct a new one. After a year, she sold the big house and bought a smaller one three doors away from the home she and Samuel had shared.

Ramona's home is a reflection of them both, a gracious home built in 1908, across the street from a sprawling city park. Clustered on the front porch are enormous coral geraniums and hibiscus whose colors mimic the roof tiles of the house. Inside, the living room is blue with white trim, has a large white brick fireplace, high ceilings, soft coral and blue furniture. A grand piano stands to one side. Fine art and antiques add grace and character to each room. Ramona has a library office, filled with books, magazines, and papers all signaling a very full life.

We talked about how one's life experiences affect the way we cope with the death of a spouse.

Ramona reflected, "Samuel assumed that he would die first, and he prepared me for being alone. He always advised me in my decisions. He often prefaced his advice with, 'If anything happens to me. . . .' He also taught me about running a house. Whenever a repair was necessary, he insisted that I watch and learn. This was a great gift, one that gave me the confidence to buy another house. I knew I could take care of it—either by myself or by calling the right people."

Now, three years after losing Samuel, Ramona could be pensive and introspective, but she was also a delightful conversationalist and great fun to be around. She was brimming with life, energy, and plans for the future.

Ramona declared, "There just isn't enough time for me to do everything I want to do! I want to take piano lessons, I want to take a drawing course. I want to travel again. And I would like to have a part-time job, but I don't know if I will be qualified."

In the fall of 1999 Ramona received three job offers, without ever applying for one. Deciding that she wanted to brush up on her Italian, in preparation for travel, Ramona called the Berlitz school. She spoke at length with the receptionist, mostly in Spanish. The woman admired Ramona's accent and her beautiful rolled r's. A few days later, the director of the school called and offered her a job teaching Spanish.

When she went to the local Blood Center to donate blood, she saw job postings, asked about openings, and was immediately offered a full-time job. When she mentioned to her financial planner that she was looking for part-time work, he offered her a job.

"You cannot imagine what this has done for me!" Ramona exclaimed. "It has boosted my self-confidence three-fold! I just couldn't believe that people would want to hire me. While I have never been unsure of myself, I think I still lacked a little self-confidence. This is so affirming. I begin my training at Berlitz on Thursday, and I am so excited about learning the methodology for teaching and then working with adults. This is tailored for me, and I am delighted."

"Are you proud of yourself?" I asked.

Her answer was strong and definite, "Yes, I am. I came through very well. We all can do so much more than we thought we were capable of. I have learned not to underestimate myself."

I asked Ramona if she had unanswered questions for her husband. "Oh, yes. I always have wondered about his antique pistol collection and how he acquired those guns. And I wonder about one other thing. Samuel was a very talkative, articulate man, but every now and then I would see a pensive, melancholy cast in his eyes, as he stared off into space. When I would ask what he was thinking about, he would say, 'You wouldn't understand.' To this day I cannot imagine what came over him. What was so intense that I wouldn't understand?" Ramona sighed softly.

Then she continued, "Samuel always wanted me to tell him stories of when I was a little girl. One story always made Samuel cry. Would you like to hear the story?"

I nodded, mesmerized by Ramona's lilting voice and poetic language.

"Where I grew up, the land and climate were much like Arizona. We had to work hard to keep up our gardens. Fog was very, very rare. One day when I was about five years old, we had a fog. Barefoot and wearing my little nightgown, I went outside. A sheet of fog enveloped our garden. I could see our neighbor's house as though through layers of cotton.

"In the afternoon I took out a little tin box. I left it in the garden overnight because I wanted to catch the fog. The next morning I rushed out to find my box and the fog I had captured. Of course there was nothing there. I remember this was the first time in my life that I was disappointed.

"Samuel loved this story and I told it to him many times. And every time I told it, he cried. How I would love to know why this touched his heart so."

As I listened, I began silently crying too, for Ramona, for Samuel, for my losses, and for the universal discovery that we cannot hold forever what is dear to us. And sometimes we cannot even capture it at all.

After a moment Ramona smiled gently. We had had our sad moment, and she was composed and happy again. I had one more question, one that seemed too obvious to ask. "On a scale of 1 to 10 for Pessimism and Optimism, where would you place yourself?"

"I think I am a 9. That is my personality, always." And Ramona's broad smile returned, dimples and all.

She paused a moment, reflecting, then added quietly, "We all think that we have ordinary lives. Then when we put it all together, we recall and realize that not one is an ordinary life at all."

CHAPTER 14

A Letter to My Husband

July 24, 1999

Dear Dick,

Today is six months since you left. Have you been watching me, have you seen my sadness, my struggles? Have you really talked to me? Do you know how much I miss you every single hour of every single day? Do you know how often you are with me, as I move about our house, and as I drive on streets we traveled together so many times?

Last night I tried to call to you in my mind. I asked, "How are you?" You answered, "Death heals all." I am waiting to be healed in this life, of my terrible grief.

Sometimes I really am okay. I stay so busy—doing, planning. I've taken several classes; I've read many books. I go out to lunch or dinner with friends. Somehow I've managed to run the house, clean out parts of the basement, donate many of your old textbooks, deal with lawyers and accountants, complete our taxes, and keep up the yard.

The flavor of everything is different now—bland, empty. I tell myself, "I'm doing this because Dick would want me to" or "Dick would be pleased." We now have a real guestroom. We. It's still We, and it is always Our house. Is thinking this way a form of denial? Maybe. Thinking of pleasing you has moved me to act more than once.

My mind plays tricks on me. When I walk in the house, I still look to see if you brought in the mail, if your briefcase is on the chair. I listen for your car in the driveway. Then I catch myself. Everything is right where I left it. What I would give to see you sitting in your lounge chair on the patio, puffing on your awful cigar, and reading your spy novel. What I would give for you to eat a dinner I spent hours cooking so that you could wink at me and say, "NTB—not too bad!"

I still cry but not as much as at first. These few months seem like five years— and also just a day or two. Was it last week, or last January, that we left so eagerly for Hawaii? How often I recall our last two days together, our shared adventures and delicious dinners in that beautiful land.

I'm not sure how the world has gone on without you. Mine stopped when yours did. Time stopped too. And then one day it began again. I'm trying so hard to continue in a way that would please you and that will bring me some joy.

All our children are thriving. Their daily lives have not been altered as mine has been. They are fine people, strong and healthy, mentally, physically, and emotionally. We can be very proud.

Thank you, dearest one, for all your gifts, for all you taught me: your resourcefulness, your analytical way of approaching business matters, your sense of humor. And thank you for sending me all the right people and the right experiences at the right times these last six months—that was your doing, wasn't it?

I am torn between believing and not believing, between wanting to believe and fearing to believe, that you are a spirit in my life, that you have a new existence in a new plane, that you see and hear me and affect my life. It is as though my right brain and my left brain are arguing and neither one can prove or disprove its argument.

You said to me at the beginning, "There is no time." I read recently that time is simply a way of marking two concurrent events. If that is so, and you are waiting for me, it really doesn't matter when we will be together again—and sometimes I think we still are. We humans put so much stock in longevity. From your vantage point, I suspect it's all vainglory. "What fools these mortals be." Is that how it seems to you?

Why doesn't love cease when the object of the love dies? Why is my heart still so full of love for you? Maybe it's because love carves an indelible home in our minds and in our spiritual hearts. Maybe it is because you are still with me and that love truly is redirected to you through time and space, even though I can't see or hold or touch you.

Please don't ever fade from my consciousness. Don't stop sending people, experiences, and messages. If that is you talking in my brain, please don't ever stop. Just thinking it's you keeps me going.

I love you. I miss you. I hope wherever you are that you are at rest and at peace.

Your wife and soulmate,
Diane

CHAPTER 15

Of Mice and (Wo)men

One day early in August, I awoke at 2 A.M. to the sound of Jennifer, my geriatric cat, speaking in tongues. Instantly I sat up and turned on the light. About three feet from my bed, on the white carpet, was Jennifer, the mighty huntress, with a mouse in her mouth. From years of reading comic books in my youth, I knew the proper incantation. I bellowed, *"Eeeeek!"* in my highest decibel. My shriek, which fell only on cat ears, shook the rafters of my house.

Oblivious, Jennifer dropped her trophy on the floor. It didn't move. Omigod, what do I do? I had crossed the minefields of house paint, wasps, taxes, gutters, and car repairs, but a *dead mouse?* Over the seven months since January, I had experienced every shade of shock, sorrow, and loneliness, but no grief group, no loving family and friends, no quiet meditations prepared me for the havoc created by a mouse in my house.

Ignoring my screams, Jennifer continued to gurgle and brag about her conquest, while I continued to shriek intermittently. In what felt like an out-of-body moment, I thought, "All this screaming would sure feel a whole lot better if somebody else could hear me!"

Collecting my wits as best I could, I weighed my options. I couldn't leave the room because Jennifer and her victim were situated on the only path from my bed to the door. It was the middle of the night so I couldn't call a neighbor. I did what any sensible woman would do. I rolled onto my stomach, pulled up the covers, and clamped a pillow over my head, squeezing a thousand feathers to my ears. A few minutes later, through the soundproofing, I heard muffled sounds of mastication. I crushed the pillow so hard, I thought my eardrums would break. In a few minutes, curiosity overcame fear, and I uncovered one ear: *slurp, munch, chomp, crunch.* I opened one eye. Jennifer was methodically devouring her quarry. The entire scene was disgusting beyond description, and I was a captive audience in my own bed. *Going undercover* took on a whole new meaning.

Submerging once more beneath my feathery fortress, I tried to look at the bright side. "Jennifer has done me two favors: 1) She caught the darned thing, and 2) She's tidying up after herself." The next time I peeked out, I caught a glimpse of Jennifer's tail as she sashayed out of the bedroom. A tiny drop of blood on the carpet was the only memento of the mighty mouser's conquest.

By 5 A.M., I had made the only sensible decision for a woman in my position: *Sell the house!* In my mousemerized brain, this was the obvious solution.

Everything looks better in daylight. The cleanup was easy, Jennifer was her old, calm self, and, of course, the intruder was gone.

A week later, in the middle of the night, Jennifer's meow once again spoke volumes to my sensitized ears. I watched as she and a gray, furry beast played cat and mouse under the furniture. Jennifer didn't attack her prey; she played with it! With her paws, she batted at the mouse repeatedly, while it raced frantically from one end of the dresser to the other. After observing this game for several minutes, I picked up a book and read. I couldn't believe I was so nonchalant! But what else

could I do? Finally the mouse scurried out of the room and into the den. From my bed I could see Jennifer sitting in her wait-and-pounce mode. Based on recent history, I was sure Jennifer would stop fooling around soon and get serious about preparing her breakfast.

Wrong. The next day I saw the mouse scamper down a hallway and disappear. A friend advised that I set a few mousetraps. In theory, that made sense, but what would I do if I actually caught it? Moreover, I had no experience with these devices. Aside from attending a performance of *The Mousetrap* in London several years ago, I was completely unqualified.

I needed to be more pro-active. In seven months I had developed a new maxim: *If you need an expert, find one.* I opened the yellow pages, where I found John the Pest Arrester. The voice on the phone was patient and sympathetic. Fortunately, this discerning man understood the gravity of the situation and was at my door within the hour. He assured me that he could get rid of the mouse. In fact, he was so confident, his service came with a 60-day guarantee that my mouse would be gone. I laughed. Would we need a little mouse ID bracelet to identify the culprit and validate the guarantee?

Our first mission was a reconnaissance of the perimeter of the house, which exposed several openings, including one large enough for a battalion of mice to enter. A tour of the basement revealed that we had had many houseguests over the years. In order to stop the assault and capture the current culprit, John caulked the openings and set out plastic bags of bait in the crawl spaces of the basement. He explained the process: the mice smell the yummy bait, ignore the *Poison* warning, gnaw open the bags, eat heartily, become ill and die.

John doesn't advocate traps because they can be high maintenance. If his customers are squeamish and can't deal with the results, he has to come back often just to empty the traps. It is easier when the mice crawl away and die. To humor me and pacify my need for visual proof, he set one trap in the room of the last sighting. I was ready to offer John my first-born child to stay for the kill, but he seemed certain that the bait, the trap, or the cat would resolve the problem. He promised that if we apprehended the villain, he would return to remove him from the trap.

That evening I was in my office on the phone with my friend Harriet, who, much to her regret, had inquired about my day. I was annotating my mouse tale, when in paraded Jennifer, this time with a mouse squirming between her teeth. I shrieked into Harriet's ear, "Jennifer's got a live mouse in her mouth! *Eeeek!*" At least this time I had an audience.

Startled, Jennifer dropped her catch, which dashed under the nearest piece of furniture. Instantly, I shut down the computer and rushed from the room, slamming the door and leaving the two adversaries to duke it out. I stuffed a towel under the door, barricading them both in the room. There would be no e-mail jokes tonight.

By 7 A.M., I was on the phone with John, my new best friend. I reported the incident and begged him to come over and check out the office with me. He appeared at 9 A.M. "Where are your weapons?" I asked. He chuckled and entered the room, unarmed. I was impressed. Probably the mouse was too, because he remained hidden, while Jennifer strolled out casually. John saw no evidence that the critter had returned. He placed a trap in the office, assuring me that a full-time sentry would only frighten the mouse and cause it to run away.

This happened to be the day of Jennifer's annual appointment with the vet. Instructions: no food for eight hours before the visit. Cute. How was I to know whether she had scarfed a snack while locked up with Mighty Mouse? When John left, I threw Jenn in the car and left for the vet. I was glad to vacate the Hot Zone for a few hours. I left Jenn at the vet's for a grooming. (In her declining years, due to either arthritis or laziness, she no longer grooms her back. Personally I consider her passive aggressive. But I digress.)

My next stop was an appointment with Sherri, my chiropractor, a delightful young woman who sympathized with my situation. "How are you going to check for the mouse?" she asked.

"I have no idea."

"Would you like me to come over later between patients and do a mouse check with you?"

"Oh, my gosh, would you really do that?"

My faith in humankind overflowed, and I made a mental note to add Sherri to my will. She appeared at 2:30. Stealthily, we eased open the door and gingerly tiptoed into the combat area, Sherri in the lead, me lagging two steps behind. The trap was empty, the bait untouched. We resealed the room.

By 5 P.M. I was nervous again. I prevailed upon my neighbor Marilyn to drop by for the next mouse patrol. Again, no catch. As a longtime homeowner, Marilyn offered an opinion. "You know, Diane, I don't think that mouse is in here. He probably was so scared that he ran away. I say you open the door and get on with your life."

Easy for her to say. I was jealous that she could go home to her husband and her mousefree environment. A little while later another friend happened to call. I explained that my house was under siege. She generously volunteered for the 8 P.M. shift. Again, no mouse.

During the night I tried some self-talk. First I asked, "Is my reaction real, is it my little-girl conditioning about mice, or am I truly afraid?"

My answer was a resounding, "Yes, yes, and yes!"

Then I tried another tack. "Diane, you are a lot bigger than that little mouse, and this is *your* house, not his. He probably has made himself a nice bait sandwich and stepped outside to turn up his little mousy paws. *Get a grip, you wimp!*" I scolded myself. For emphasis, I added the immortal words of Joan Rivers, "*Grow up!* "

By the next morning, I had convinced myself that the danger was greatly diminished, that Mr. Mouse had probably checked out by now. Besides, how long could I live like this, unable to visit my computer, my checkbook, and my copy machine? Was I a (wo)man or a mouse? I dismantled the barricades to the office, turned on my computer, and announced in stentorian tones, "Okay, mouse, I'm back. You're history. This is my house, and you're not getting rid of me so fast!"

In matters of survival, I subscribe to the school of *More is more*. That afternoon, feeling strong, I marched into the drug store to purchase more mouse-traps, artillery for the next skirmish. With four packs of traps in hand, I marched to the checkout. Smiling pleasantly, I asked the young man at the register, "Can you show me how to set this mousetrap?"

"Who, me? No, ma'am. I have no idea. My Dad does all that kind of stuff." Just what I needed to hear: this is man's work. I felt an ugly twinge.

Frustrated, I asked, "Well, isn't there anyone in the store who can help me? You sell these traps. Somebody here must know how to use them. It can't be that complicated."

The lady manager appeared. Written all over her smug face was "Yuck!" Her sour look said, "Tsk, tsk. And in such a nice neighborhood. Some housekeeper you must be." She gave me a scornful glance, shrugged, and muttered something about good luck. I left the store with four useless mousetraps.

When I reached the parking lot, I began to sob. I felt as alone as at any time in the past seven months. I could not believe I was having a meltdown over a stupid mouse. I had tried valiantly to handle the situation, had gotten professional help, had not dissolved into a helpless puddle—until now. My cat was unreliable at best; I had imposed enough upon the good natures of my friends. I dreaded returning home and facing another night alone. I felt helpless and full of self-pity.

Pulling myself together, I went to pick up Jennifer. I must have looked terrible because the receptionist asked if I was okay. On the verge of tears, I told her my sad tale. Where can you find empathy for an animal story if not at the veterinary clinic? Miraculously, this lovely lady turned out to be an expert on mousetraps, and she showed me exactly what to do. I was empowered!

Giving each trap a dab of peanut butter, I placed one in the kitchen and one in the laundry room, out of Jenn's reach. I was sure that I was the only female in the county with the mousing skills I now possessed.

Days passed with no further signs of mice, and I began to believe that the bait was working. Of course, I never went to the basement unaccompanied, in case a mouse had expired on the premises. Visiting workmen removed one or two carcasses, which made me feel good—sort of. As a precaution, I heralded my nocturnal trips to the bathroom with Sound and Light shows, warnings that Big Foot was coming. My mouse, which had assumed giant proportions in my mind, was now only about two feet long and shrinking daily. Two weeks went by. The traps were untouched, and I had had no more sightings.

Soon it was fall, the season when mouse families gather to make big deci-sions about real estate. "There's a nice house. Good eats. Let's winter there. C'mon, kids." I hoped the caulking would do the job and that the mouse popula-tion would look elsewhere for their winter homes.

During the mouse saga, I had a few epiphanies. First, I understood why women want to marry. It is no cosmic coincidence that Mouse, House, and Spouse not only rhyme; they are inextricably bound together in the web of life.

On the practical side, I now knew how to set a mousetrap. I also knew when and how to call John the Pest Arrester. If my mouse, or any of his kin, returned, I would scream and shriek—that's in my genes—but I would not become undone.

In his poem *To a Mouse* [4] written in 1785, the Scottish poet Robert Burns wrote, "The best laid schemes o' mice and men gang oft a-gley; an' lea'e us nought but grief and pain for promis'd joy." Grief and pain had indeed replaced promised joy for me. And certainly my plans had "gang a-gley." My plans never included losing my husband and our life together. I never planned to shoulder all the responsibilities of home-ownership by myself. I never planned to have a mouse in my house. It seemed that every day brought some unanticipated problem. How many times and in how many ways must I be tested? After seven months of hurdles, just as I thought my universe was coming under control, a tiny creature sent me into a spiral of fear and despair.

Yet, this little fellow taught me a few lessons. I learned that I could fall apart, cry, feel sorry for myself—and then turn around and tackle the problem from a new perspective. I discovered that I was stronger and more resourceful than I had ever realized. I learned that fear was manageable and that while I was not always victorious, I was also not easily defeated. I had met one more challenge in my new life. I was proud of myself.

And I learned that keeping my sense of humor was the only way through this world. Dick always knew that. I was sure that during the mouse saga, he was cheering me on. Now we could laugh about it together. It was almost the way it used to be.

But not quite.

CHAPTER 16

A Wedding in Jerusalem

In August my nephew Michael would be married in Israel. Michael is studying to be a Conservative rabbi and has made *aliyah:* he has become an Israeli citizen. His bride Tamar is also a student of Judaica. Her family lives in Jerusalem.

Could I travel so far by myself? And how would I handle this first wedding? I dreaded the trip and would gladly have stayed home, but this was my only sibling's child. I had to be there.

When my brother David and his wife Anne generously invited me to join them, first spending a week in Switzerland, I was reluctant. My friends urged me to go. I wouldn't be alone and it could be fun. I finally decided to go. It would be hard, but I would just do it. When I mentioned the trip to my friend Susan, she said, "I've always dreamed of going to Switzerland!" And so we became a foursome. Susan and I would spend a few extra days in Switzerland, and then I would fly alone to Israel.

What follows is from my travel journal. We left on Monday, August 2, and returned on Friday, August 20.

ଓଃ ଓଃ ଓଃ

Thursday, August 5, 1999: The flights were fine, but I hate maneuvering luggage myself. We have spent two pleasant days in Lucerne.

This is so hard. Everything was so much easier at home, in my house, my town, and my day-to-day life. I need to try to enjoy more or at least not be negative. I need Shari's attitude, "Don't be a sad-sack and have other people think you're a pain in the you-know-what." The others have no idea how torturous this is for me. They talk about their lives like nothing in this world has changed.

How terribly I miss Dick. We always enjoyed traveling to new places and having adventures. I keep thinking, "Dick would have loved this. Why can't he be here to experience this?"

I feel terribly alone, even with three other people. I find myself thinking of Dick even more than at home—or perhaps just with greater pain.

It helps to have Susan along. I feel less like a fifth wheel. There is no resolution for my aching except crying—and trying not to cry around the others. The trip is hard in ways I didn't anticipate. Does this mean no trips in the future? Guess I'd best not think about that and try to adapt.

Maybe I am just over-tired and will come back to myself tomorrow when we go hiking in the mountains.

Friday, August 6, 1999: We are in Zermatt, the town at the foot of the Matterhorn. Hotel is dreary. Last night Susan and I had separate rooms and it was terrible for me. When I closed the door of my dark, depressing room and faced the silence, I was entirely alone in a foreign land.

I crawled onto the bed and sobbed until I felt empty. I was weeping for all our happy times in beautiful places, for this lovely trip that Dick was missing, for my aloneness. I remembered, "Experience it all for me." I cried even harder.

In my sleep/non-sleep state, I spoke to Dick. And I received an answer, "Put me in a secret corner of your heart and mind. I am with you. Try to enjoy this."

Today was much better for me. When I woke up, I told myself, "You'd better start enjoying this. Don't spoil everyone else's trip. Buck up, lady!" I prayed for strength.

During our hike, one of the women accidentally called David "Dick"—and gasped. But it was okay.

Our hiking was rigorous and we were very high up in the mountains. In my head I said to Dick, "You would never have been able to walk this, so I'm taking you on my shoulder. I'll do all the work." I put Dick in a special place in my heart, and my little secret felt good.

I don't feel much like collecting souvenirs—who will I share them with?

Maybe the rest of the trip will be easier in some ways without David and Anne, constant reminders of couplehood and what I so recently had. They really are fun to be with and are trying to make this a great time.

Maybe all the exercise, fresh air, walking, and sightseeing have energized and toughened me a little. I'm glad to be here and to be feeling a little better.

Saturday, August 7, 1999: Rigorous day: long drive to Grindelwald near the famous Jungfrau.

Scenery is unbelievable. It appears that Switzerland had one architect who designed one chalet—dark wood, red-brown roof, geraniums in every window—and everyone else in the country followed suit. Why tamper with success? The effect is quaint and lovely. Long, long hike today. Went into town—this is Gatlinburg with watches!

Sunday, August 8, 1999: Today we climbed the Jungfrau. Well, we didn't exactly climb it. We were up at 5:30 for a 7:19 train right outside our hotel. Two trains, 9000 bridges and tunnels, and a 50-degree drop in temperature later, we arrived in clouds at the Jungfrau Station. Amazing! What a thrill—this is truly the Roof of the World, the Top of Europe.

We wanted to take a dogsled ride but the snow was too soft so we walked around outside—very warm when the sun came out. Everything in sight is white; air is crystal clear, and the sky is cobalt blue.

After lunch, Anne and David drove Susan and me to Interlochen, where we boarded the train for the hour ride to Berne. Took a long walk in the shopping arcades of this lovely city.

Monday, August 9, 1999: Wonderful City Tour, beginning with visit to the top of the famous clock tower. We were there at noon when little wooden bears, chickens, and jesters marked the hour, while crowds watched from the street far below. We were on the inside watching this amazing Rube Goldberg-type mechanical clockworks, invented by a blacksmith in the 14-15th century. Dick would have loved it and understood all the engineering involved.

Walked around the Old City, which was founded in 1191, burned in 1405, and rebuilt in sandstone. Somehow Berne missed the Renaissance, so it remains very much an old medieval town.

Tuesday, August 10, 1999: Traveled to Basel, which is noisy, congested, and not nearly so charming as Berne.

Wednesday, August 11, 1999: Day of Solar Eclipse. We sat in front of the hotel as the sky grew dark. Ate lunch on the train to Zurich Airport.

Lost Susan for nearly two hours in the airport. Became panicky. Went to Information desk and eventually to police. I even spoke into the PA system, calling for her. Finally found her in the train station section of the Airport. A pretty natural mistake but a frightening experience. I hugged her like crazy and cried with relief!

Checked our luggage through for tomorrow's flights. When I told the woman at the El Al desk of my terrible day, she upgraded me to Business Class. Ah, the kindness of strangers!

Had a great Italian dinner in the picturesque little town near the airport. What a charming surprise! We walked for hours, admiring the barn-houses, with trailing flowers in every window, nook, and cranny; green green grass, delightful vegetable and flower gardens, wide fields of corn, tiny church and school, and more cows than in all of Wisconsin.

Thursday, August 12, 1999: It was hard to tell Susan good-bye. I'll miss her. Can't imagine this trip without her smile and fun-loving good nature. We spent a lot of time doing hair and make-up—there are some advantages in traveling with a woman. She understands why it takes so long in the bathroom!

Flew to Tel Aviv by myself. For once I would have liked a chatty seatmate. Cried a little several times—I needed a good cry—tears of sadness, self-pity, and loneliness. I couldn't help but recall how Dick and I had traveled here together only nine months ago.

One day as we were riding along silently, I recalled a conversation I had overheard in a restaurant a few weeks before. Two women were discussing the challenges they were confronting in their lives. One of them declared that her toughest challenge was working her computer. I thought a lot about that comment. Every day is hard for me, and the next nine days will present new tests: my first international travel alone; my first wedding alone, with no access to my car to escape when I might need to; no one of kindred spirit who can understand how difficult this is for me. How I yearn for a time when the computer will be my greatest challenge!

Meanwhile, I pray for strength to get through all this without breaking down, without feeling too sad.

Took so long to clear customs that my luggage carousel was no longer marked. Finally found my stuff. Long, hot drive in a crowded van to Jerusalem and to the hotel, which is awful. No one to help with my luggage. Room is on floor 6-1/2, with no elevator from 6 to 6-1/2. Weird. Long hike, dragging my luggage up steps. No way to connect my hair dryer, no towels. Sink is as big as a breadbox. And this is called a Suite—home for my daughter and me for a week. I was nearly in tears. Physically and emotionally this has been rough.

At the time that Margie was due to arrive in Tel Aviv, she called from Milwaukee. Her flight was canceled and she will be a day late. Poor kid.

Went to dinner with a large family group, about 20 men, women, and noisy teenagers. It was okay. I managed to converse with people but felt completely on the outside.

I cannot *wait* to go home. Seven more days.

Friday, August 13, 1999: Margie arrived exhausted and with a terrible headache.

Did some touring, walked on the ramparts of Old City, South wall excavations. Made it a special point to visit the Hurva Synagogue, because of what Paulette had told me, but nothing happened. It is hot beyond hot—probably close to 100 degrees, maybe 95 in the sparse but welcome shade.

Pre-nuptial Shabbat service, all in Hebrew of course. This was very hard for me. Tears are always so close: all these grandparents, all these big families, and every woman with a husband. It hurts so much.

Went to the bride's home for a Chinese dinner. Everyone is very nice, but even in a crowd, I feel so isolated. And yet, how could I not be here?

Cute slide show of Michael and Tamar's lives.

This celebration of love and marriage is more than I can bear.

And the hotel is a pit. Who chose this place?

Saturday, August 14, 1999: We all went to a Shabbat service. Michael and Tamar and some family members read. There was a lengthy Bar Mitzvah all in Hebrew, naturally. Couldn't *wait* to get out.

Went to a lovely brunch at the grandparents' home. Lots of food, kids lolling around. Margie and I sat on one side, spoke to a few people. Hot day.

I feel so much on the outside of all this joy, so joyless inside myself. I wish the young couple well, am happy for their love, and imagine their life together will be a good one. It is hard work trying to be pleasant and keep smiling. This event isn't about me, and I know that, but I can't turn off my own surging emotions.

Margie suggested that we go to dinner alone instead of with the large group—a "mother and daughter bonding dinner." She selected the restaurant, found our way there with her map. It was delicious and lovely. And it was a great relief to have someone else in charge. I loved being alone with my daughter. Margie was chatty and we had a good time together. How does she always know what I need?!

It was my best two hours so far in Jerusalem.

Switzerland and the trip here were more grueling than I realized.

Finally, the hotel has agreed to move Margie and me both to single rooms.

Five more full days. Dear God, please give me strength and make the time pass quickly.

Sunday, August 15, 1999: A large group went to Masada—in 100 degrees. Because I had been there, I joined Anne's parents on a long walk. Excellent tour of the Supreme Court—amazing building with curves and lines, representing justice and law, lights, pyramids, circles. More touring. Hot, tired, but enjoyed the companionship of these two upbeat, energetic people.

Dinner at vegetarian restaurant. I like that.

Not a bad day. New room is small but much better. It even has a counter in the bathroom!

I'm doing okay now—a few sad moments. Still dread the wedding. Michael had asked me to stand under the *chuppah* (bridal canopy) and read a passage, but I declined. I just can't do it. How could I risk falling apart in front of all those people?

Monday, August 16, 1999: Spent some time with Michael, went to a mall where we chose a pearl ankle bracelet for Tamar.

I asked him what he remembered of his visit with Dick when we were in Israel last November.

"We were walking to or from the restaurant, and Dick asked that we take a cab. He explained that walking, especially on the hills, was hard for him—hard breathing. He didn't apologize. He just said he couldn't do the walking. He told me, 'I live my life from day to day, knowing that I could go any moment. I do what I want to do because of that.'"

This took my breath away. Dick had never told me how closely he lived with thoughts of his own death. I must think about this.

Told Michael how hard this trip is for me. Shared with him all the mystical things that have happened, and how my left and right brains argue. Then I told him about our visit to Mt. Nebo last year, when the tour guide asked Dick to read the passage about Moses' death. I remember that Dick was deeply shaken in a way I had never seen.

Michael told me a story about a woman named Rachel, an Israeli pioneer, who because of her tuberculosis was unable to fulfill her dream of working on the land at her kibbutz. Instead she became a poet, who wrote of her longing for a child and for her lost dreams. On her tombstone is a line from her poetry, "Every person has his Mt. Nebo."

Ah, don't we?

I cried. Michael is young but sensitive. I think he understood. He said it had never occurred to him that the wedding might be difficult for me. I explained about the many, many layers and the terrible moments when all the pain surfaces. If sensitive Michael was unaware of my turmoil, how could I expect anyone else to understand? I guess sympathy is one thing, empathy something else. Walk a mile in my shoes.

Am reading *Widowed* by Dr. Joyce Brothers [5], whose husband Milt died of cancer at 62. Here is someone who understands. This was the right book to bring along. She says that people cope best who have faced other trials before and have built some inner strength. Many of the families here have never known rain in their lives. I don't resent their good fortune—I envy it.

Margie and I are doing well on the trip. She loves to explore on her own. She brought back stones from Masada to place on the two graves, of her dad and Dick.

Dinner with 20 happy people was hard. I become very quiet. Someone asked me, "Are you okay?"

"Sure," I answered, "I'm just tired."

I heard Erik, my niece Marjorie's husband, call her "Sweetie." I need more glue.

Last night I called out to Dick. He said, "My love is real (Is-real?)." Is this one of Dick's puns? I chuckled silently.

Tuesday, August 17, 1999: Margie and I went with Erik to the Old City, from 9 A.M. to 2 P.M. in sweltering heat. What a sweaty mass of humanity.

The wedding was on the campus of Hebrew Union College, where Michael and Tamar studied and where her father is a member of the faculty. Jerusalem at dusk is so beautiful, truly Jerusalem of the Gold, with the lights dancing on the ancient walls and buildings. From the campus one looks across a valley to the Old City—what a spectacular view.

I recalled the moment when Dick and I arrived in Israel. The El Al plane touched the ground and all the passengers spontaneously began to sing "Hatikva," the Israeli national anthem. I looked over and saw Dick wiping his eyes. I remember that Dick seemed a little embarrassed by his emotions. "I don't know why I'm reacting this way," he had said.

The wedding festivities began with an hour of picture-taking in a lovely courtyard garden. Then came the *ketubbah* ceremony, signing of the legal documents that seal the marriage. Michael and Tamar presented a lengthy philosophical discussion for this occasion.

Again I felt on the outside of everything.

There followed an hour-long reception for the 200+ guests, again endless to me. We sat down, and I choked back tears several times. One high spot. I met a distant branch of my dad's family that lives in Israel. Lovely people, and one of the little girls looks like old pictures of me!

Finally the ceremony. Margie and I sat in back and cried through most of the service. Seeing young love, hearing vows of commitment, feeling the joy of bride and groom, seeing souls and hands touching were very difficult. I was happy for Michael and Tamar, two wonderful young people. But nothing could assuage my own pain. Even the beauty of Jerusalem could not console me.

After the ceremony, we moved to a large courtyard for a buffet dinner. I was seated at a large, round table with four married couples. When the dancing began, right on cue they all waltzed away to the dance floor, leaving me absolutely alone.

Each of my widowed friends had had the identical experience at a wedding. Knowing what to expect lent a note of dark humor and easier acceptance. I took a moment to feel sorry for myself, then stood up and went to join Margie at her table, where the same exodus had occurred.

The moment passed, as did the wedding. We were able to leave the celebration early, and no one questioned us. We came back to the hotel and I fell apart.

I miss Dick so much. No matter how hard I try, I can't make him be here.

Wednesday, August 18, 1999: WE LEAVE TOMORROW!

I have made it! But none of this trip was easy.

Will the challenges never end?

I feared this trip would be difficult and it was. I spent many months dreading this event, punishing myself with anticipated pain. To my surprise, my apprehension lasted far longer than the event. The wedding was over in a matter of a few hours. It was bittersweet, like so much else these days.

Being here was not a choice for me. I am glad I came. Maybe in comparison, future challenges will seem less enormous. I have passed another hurdle.

The saying "This too shall pass" refers not only to joyous times, which fly by too quickly, but also to the difficult moments. Inexorably, time does pass.

Tomorrow I go home. The house will be empty, but I will be glad to be there. It is home.

CHAPTER 17

In the Winepress

The Lord hath trodden under foot all my mighty men in the midst of me:
He hath called an assembly against me to crush my young men: the Lord
hath trodden the virgin, the daughter of Judah, as in a winepress.
[Lamentations 1:15].

From the moment I met Hannah Lemke, I sensed a rare and exquisite quality. She is a beautiful woman with soft, curly white hair, bright hazel eyes, and classic features. But Hannah is so much more: she is radiant. An aura of goodness and love surround her, a warm glow of calm, acceptance, zest, and spirit. She exudes energy and joy in living.

An only child, she was born Hannah Schmitt in Kassel, Germany in 1941. When Hannah was ten, her parents immigrated to Wilmette, Illinois, where her dad's brother lived.

Eric Lemke was born in Berlin in 1939. His father was a prisoner of war in Siberia for many years, leaving his mother to raise Eric and his twin brother. Early in the war, the three of them fled to Poland. After the Russian advance, the family fled back to a burnt-out Berlin. In 1957, when Eric was 18, he arrived in Chicago with a suitcase in his hand. A friend sponsored him, and he began working in construction, steel, and mechanical drawing. At night he took engineering courses at Northwestern University. For fun he played soccer on a Swedish soccer team.

One night Hannah attended a soccer match with friends. There she met Eric, a handsome young man of 20, to Hannah's 17. After that evening, Hannah never dated anyone else. The two fell deeply in love. In 1961, just before Hannah's twentieth birthday, they were married. For the next 37 years, they were soulmates.

In high school Hannah had taken business courses; after graduation she found an excellent job with an insurance firm in the Loop in Chicago. Six months after the wedding, Eric was called into the service. Vicenza, Italy, just outside Venice, was their home for two years, and their daughter Lisa was born there in 1963. The family lived off the army post in a charming place. Hannah considered this time a great experience for them all.

After the service, back in Chicago, Eric began working as a draftsman at a construction company. Eric Jr. was born in 1965. Two years later Eric accepted a job with another construction company, this time in Milwaukee, where he did estimating, consulting, and engineering work. A loyal, dedicated, hard-working employee, Eric remained with the company for his entire career.

Even as I entered the Lemke home, on Milwaukee's West Side, I felt the love that must have filled it every day since 1967. Hannah opened the door and the aroma of warm apples and cinnamon greeted me. On the stove was a beautiful French apple pie, which Hannah had baked just for our visit. Over green tea and pie this gentle lady told me of the life she had lived, with the man she loves and misses every day of her life.

Always a strong and healthy man, in the fall of 1997 Eric began to have stomach discomfort. Strangely, he could not tolerate odors and would have to leave the house when Hannah cooked. Eric looked fine and generally felt well. The doctors treated him for an ulcer.

When the symptoms persisted, Eric went for an ultrasound. Eric Jr., now an intern at the medical college, stood with the technician who gave the test. As he watched the screen, the young man could not believe what he saw. On his father's liver and pancreas were cancerous tumors.

The doctors gave Eric two to three months to live.

Hannah said, "When Eric came home from the test, he took me in his arms and said, 'Honey, God will help us through this,' and we clung to each other. We had always had great faith in God, and we knew that our faith would sustain us."

In the first days after the cancer diagnosis, realizing what lay ahead, Hannah remembered Jesus' last days in Gethsemane, when he had to drink the cup of bitter water, a symbol of what he must go through. "This bitter cup was now before me and Eric. We must drink this too. There was no way around it. And we did none of it alone. God was our strength."

To supplement the chemotherapy, which Eric sustained very well, Hannah and Eric explored alternative treatments. Hannah showed me her collection of books on alternative medicine, adjacent to many books on faith. The Lemkes followed recommended diets and used supplements, minerals, vitamins, and special teas.

During Eric's illness, their many circles of friends offered constant support, encouragement, and prayer. Two church groups held healing services for Eric.

Hannah told me, "Twice he was anointed with oil, once in a prayer meeting in a friend's home and once in our church. Everyone laid hands on him and prayed for him. We truly felt the presence of God. It was powerful. Over the months there was so much prayer. The Lord was our strength through all our trials. And Eric lived a wonderful year. We played golf, we traveled, and we were in activities at church. We enjoyed the whole summer and fall. I know that the special care, the foods, and the prayers extended his life and helped him to feel well enough to enjoy this time."

Within a few months, Eric began to have problems with his hip. A bone scan revealed that the cancer was in his bones. Eventually it entered his brain. Fortunately, Eric only had pain and suffering in the last two weeks. On March 28, 1998, Eric passed away, many months past the predicted time.

When Eric died, Hannah became the rock of her family, the one who held up everyone else. "This probably happened because I was numb and in shock. Also I had grieved before. I was the strong one for the family. Everyone leaned on me. When my children asked how I could do this, I answered, 'I've had to release your dad to God. I released him a month or two ago.'

"Two or three months later, after being so strong for everyone else, the pain and the reality threw me over. The emotions came flooding in, head to toe. Then the tears really started."

"How did you move through that terrible time?" I asked.

"I kept myself very busy. At first time seemed warped. Sometimes I simply was not all there. I was walking in a fog. Even going to the grocery store was difficult. Why was I buying food? I didn't care about food. Why would I shop just for me? Once I just threw a few things in the basket and fled the store."

A month later Hannah knew she must help herself. She enrolled in a course in Old Testament law and a computer class. She had always loved taking courses and needed to keep her mind challenged.

In the summer Hannah slowed down, occupying her time with gardening and golf, two favorite pastimes. "I have wonderful family and friends. That summer, everyone kept me busy. I had standing appointments for dinners on Tuesdays or lunches on Fridays. I was so grateful to be occupied."

Hannah has three grandchildren who adored *Opa,* their grandfather. Lovingly she showed me the pictures of the adorable children who call her *Oma, grandmother.*

"I took the children one at a time for four days. We went to the zoo, to concerts. We went hiking, swimming. I even introduced my grandson to golf, and I took the girls to mini-golf. They are such a joy, and I am so blessed to have them. Children are so wonderful."

The changing of seasons brought a new surge of emotions and new challenges for filling time. When fall came, Hannah was invited to join a choir. Although she always enjoyed singing, she had never sung in a formal setting. Two hundred people from seven area churches, including outlying areas and the inner city, would present a special Christmas concert called *Together for Christmas.*

"For the first time in my life, I joined a choir," Hannah reflected. "It was absolutely wonderful. At the end we were rehearsing seven nights a week and I loved every minute! It brought me such joy to sing, to celebrate the birth of our Lord. This was a whole new thing that God gave me to enjoy. The concert was so wonderful, so fulfilling, so joyous."

November and December had always been busy, happy months of celebration and many family birthdays: Eric, Eric Jr., and two grandchildren. That year, the holidays, the birthdays, the concert raised Hannah's spirits and kept her more than busy.

Then came January. "It was like a crash. I went into a terrible depression. I would try reading the psalms, and then I would hear myself crying out like King David did. I was on my knees, my face on the floor. I cried out to God, 'If I must be in such pain, then please, take my life. I don't want to live.'"

Taking a deep breath, Hannah continued, "God told me to go for counseling, and He led me to a person who specialized in bereavement counseling. It was she who helped me overcome the depression. She explained that this was my reaction to an accumulation of two years of heartache, first dealing with the cancer, then with Eric's death. She put me on a very low dosage of medication. After only three days, it helped me. She also urged me to keep a journal, which was difficult for me, but that helped, too.

"I only saw her four times over four weeks. Toward the end she asked me to paint some pictures for her. Twenty-five years ago I had begun to do watercolors, and I loved that. Now she was encouraging me to paint again. It was a delight for me to go back to my painting. After four weeks, she told me, 'You're fine.' I will always be grateful to that wonderful woman. She gave me hope again and helped me to deal with the heartache." Hannah's eyes glowed as she recalled the counselor's help.

Then she continued, "I faced the darkness with God. He has given me such power, comfort, peace, and strength. I often pick up the Scriptures and read psalms or the New Testament. When all the visitors have left, and you've hung up from the last phone call, you're alone. And that is when I need God."

Her voice took on a stronger tone, "I just don't want ever to go back into that dark pit of despair. Wallowing in self-pity can lead there, and I will never do that. I try to have an attitude of gratitude by counting my blessings every day. And I tell my children and my married friends to appreciate their spouses now."

After therapy, Hannah found that she began to enjoy life again. She returned to activities she had liked. Every fall she and Eric made jelly. A year and a half after her husband died, Hannah took out all the supplies and set to work. As she measured and prepared, she looked up, grinned, and said to Eric, "Honey, I know you're watching me. Am I doing it right?"

Always involved in projects, Hannah decided to redecorate the den. Eric had been devoted to the 1970's rust carpet. Now Hannah completely redid the room. She painted the room herself, two walls a day. She selected a creamy Berber carpet, refinished an old desk, purchased a new love seat, installed bookshelves, and hung one of her own paintings in the room.

"I loved doing the work. It kept me busy and productive. And now I enjoy my special little room. I even think Eric would approve. I have found that what I did before, I do again, and I add new things, all of which I enjoy thoroughly. Life is so full of exciting and wonderful things. I always like to be current in the world, to know about the news, to keep up. I think this is important. I am still very much in this world. That's why I bought a computer."

Recently, Hannah took an eight-week course in watercolors. She devotes time to her singing, and she mentors others. Hannah continues golfing. She is also involved with her mom and dad, her children and grandchildren. She has kept the family cabin in northern Wisconsin and likes hiking and mushroom-picking. She volunteers at her church, where she meets many wonderful people.

Hannah and I talked about the grieving process. When she told me that several times she has started crying while driving alone in her car, I told her about my meltdowns. How could the simple act of driving become an emotional experience? Perhaps it was because we all spend so many hours in our cars, usually alone. Being encased in that mechanical fortress—moving through time and space hearing only white noise—underscored our aloneness. For Hannah and me, the empty seat was a constant reminder of the men who had always been beside us, talking, advising, and joking. No wonder we cried.

"Would you ever remarry?" I asked. "If Robert Redford knocked on your door, would you go?"

Hannah grinned, "You bet I would!" Then she became more serious. "I have thought about it. I believe that if it is God's purpose, then it will happen. I think I would like that."

I admired Hannah's honesty about Mr. Redford and her complete comfort in God's plan for her. Her love for Eric was not diminished. This gregarious, loving person had been alone, had been tested, and she was open to future companionship and happiness in her life.

We talked about the difference between grieving and self-pity. Her comment struck a chord. "My prayer is that I will not be so self-absorbed with my tragedy that I will be blind to others. We hurt ourselves if we wallow in our grief. It's when we help others that we begin to heal. I find now that I can offer comfort and strength to others. I understand their grief. I tell them that it is okay to cry, that they need to grieve, and the tears need to come because they are healing tears."

Hannah spoke again of her deep religious faith, "I just keep on in my walk of trust with a belief in things we cannot see. Eric and I were always believers, and we knew that God would unfold step-by-step His plans for us. I know that Eric and I will be together again. We believe in the resurrection, and we have the hope of eternal life. We have a spirit, a soul. The body holds us together, but our soul lives forever. I believe God has a purpose and a plan for each one of our lives. With all we went through, I still don't know God's purpose, but I have faith in His wisdom." How moved I was by such stunning faith.

I asked Hannah if she had had any unusual experiences. "Something incredible did happen. I want to show you something." She left the table, went into another room and returned with a Bible. She opened easily to Jeremiah, Chapter 29, verse 12, where God tells the prophet that He has "plans for you." The lines were underlined and highlighted.

"See," said Hannah, "God has a purpose for us all."

I looked at the inscription inside the back cover. The date was September 11, 1995, long before Eric was ill. "That was a Saturday, early in the morning, 6:25 A.M. I had a beautiful dream of a heavenly painting, so glorious, such warmth and joy and peace. I will never forget that dream. It was so powerful that I entered the date in my Bible."

The second inscription was dated September 11, 1998, six months after Eric's death. "Just before dawn on a Saturday morning, I had my first dream about Eric. He was sitting in the den with light glowing all around him. He was talking to me, laughing, happy and healthy. I almost sensed his presence. It was so real to me. The only thing he said was, 'I'm doing wonderful.'

"I woke up and cried. I think he must be in a place like the one in my first dream. I called my children and told them, 'Dad came to me in the most wonderful way.' When I entered the date of this dream in my Bible, I was amazed to see that it was also September 11. I still wonder what the meaning of that is."

I asked Hannah if she and Eric had ever talked about how her life would be after he was no longer here. "It was too painful to talk about. We cried together. In truth we had the time but not the moment. But we did plan his memorial service together, the songs, and the passages to be read.

"On the Wednesday morning before he died, I went into the bedroom, kissed Eric good morning and said 'I love you.' He looked up, smiled, and said, 'Good morning. I love you, too.' Those were the last words he ever said."

The doorbell rang. A neighbor had come by to show Hannah a bridesmaid's dress she had sewn. It was time for me to leave. Spontaneously, Hannah and I reached out and hugged each other. We both expressed delight at the bond we had created on this lovely morning. We had laughed and cried together. I had so much to learn from this lady.

As I drove away, I recalled a comment Hannah made at the beginning of our visit. She had smiled. "We don't know what we can do until we are put in the winepress. In the face of devastation, when our spirits are broken, even then something good will come to bless others. We experience healing; we are restored.

From the terrible press flows the wine to nourish others. God has given me the strength and peace to give comfort to others."

As I settled into my car, I sighed heavily and thought of all the other women who had lost their mates. Hadn't we all been in the winepress?

God does have a purpose for each of us. Part of that purpose, one that we can know, is that He sends us the people we need at the right moment. On that October morning, He had sent me Hannah Lemke, a new and special friend, and she had nourished my soul.

CHAPTER 18

Emit the Bear

When Sue lost Jake on May 6, 1999, she was shocked and bereft, just as I had been four months earlier.

Originally Sue Gibson and I met at my daughter's wedding in 1994. Sue was with Jake and was shy and reticent around our family. We met again at Bruce's wedding in 1998. We liked and respected each other as acquaintances but we had no special relationship. Since Jake died, Sue and I had a special connection, which we nurtured through frequent long distance calls. She too had lost the love of her life, and my heart ached for her.

The possible awkwardness of knowing that she was grieving for the man I had been married to for sixteen years never existed between us. We shared an honesty that allowed her to say, "I had a terrible week. I couldn't stop crying," and me to say, "I don't know why today was so hard. I feel so vulnerable."

We understood each other as no one else could. We talked about our experiences, mundane and mystical, shared books, and tested out our reactions and our feelings because we had become sisters, in fact nearly twins, in our experience of sudden loss. Such ironies in our lives.

Sue is a pretty, petite, blond woman of about 50 with a neat page boy haircut, large blue eyes and the most beautiful, smooth, creamy complexion. She speaks in a quiet, measured, almost rhythmical cadence. Sue is one of God's gentle, soft creatures, whose sweetness and humanity are genuine and appealing. She has not one whit of guile, anger, or pettiness.

Sue and Jake were together for seventeen years, enclosed in a private world of their own design. Each of them collected porcelain figurine animals: Jake, owls; Sue, Panda bears of every size and shape. Owls and bears adorned their home.

It seemed that each time I spoke with Sue, she would tell me a story that touched me deeply and taught me more about life. A month after Jake died, Sue told me of her visit to the cemetery a few days before.

135

"I stood at Jake's grave and I cried out, 'Jake, please just give me a sign to get me through another day.' At that moment I looked down on the ground and I saw a tiny flat pebble. On the surface was a little smiley face, etched by grains of dust. When I picked it up, of course the face went away. It was only dust. I took the pebble home and painted a smiley face on it. It was a better day."

Sue and Jake loved planting flowers. Every year around Memorial Day, they would fill two large brown pots, usually with geraniums.

"This year I just wasn't in the mood." Sue told me. "Finally about mid-July, I was tired of looking at those empty pots. Suddenly Jake came into my head and said, 'Put lavender in those pots. You love lavender.' I went to the garden store and bought lavender plants. They flourished. Now it's fall, and I have replanted the flowers in the ground so they will come up next year. I think of them as Jake's flowers."

When Dick died, the rabbi warned me that sometimes about three months after the death of a loved one, survivors experience a renewed period of extreme grief, just when they seem to be adjusting to their new lives. In August, Sue told me that she was having a rough time, feeling sad and lonely, crying without warning, and missing Jake terribly. I recalled how difficult my March had been.

Sue told me of a conversation she had had with a friend. "I said to him, 'The girl I was before is lost. She's gone.'"

I asked quietly, "Who will take her place, Sue?"

She pondered the question, then replied softly, "A new girl is coming out, a mature woman. This will be a different maturity because I have weathered a different kind of storm. If I had never experienced losing Jake, this new me would never have come into being."

One day during these difficult weeks, Sue received a catalogue of collectibles. When she opened the magazine, on the first page was a soft, brown stuffed bear about two feet tall, called The Listener. The caption under the bear said, "Talk to the Listener. Tell him all your problems and all your joys. He will hear you and you will feel happy."

Sue said, "As soon as I read the description, I knew I needed a Listener, that I must have this bear. I would think of Jake's spirit as being in this big cuddly fellow and I would always have him here with me."

When the bear arrived, Sue told him that she was sending Jake's spirit to be inside him. Every night she placed the bear on her bed. He sat with her as she ate or watched TV. Each day she became more and more attached. When Sue decided that she wanted a name for her new friend, she mentioned this to her sister, who had a suggestion. "I think you should call the bear Emit, which is Time spelled backwards. Where Jake is now, Time really is kind of backwards. And it is eternal."

And so Emit became Sue's constant companion that she talked to, cried to, and loved. "You know, I feel so silly sometimes," Sue confessed to me. "But he does give me some comfort, and I really feel that Jake's spirit is here." She hesitated, then asked, "Do you think people would think I'm crazy, talking to a stuffed bear?"

Across the miles, I answered, "I think the only people who might not understand would be people who have never grieved for someone they loved. And after all, he is called the Listener. You have given yourself a wonderful gift. I am happy for you."

Sue seemed relieved. "Oh, good. Thank you for saying that!"

Then Sue told me how she longed to dream of Jake. "In all this time, I had never dreamed about Jake. I thought it would be so wonderful, almost like a visit. One night I was hugging Emit when I heard a voice in my head saying, 'If only I could dream about Jake.' That night I had a dream, and there was Jake, wearing a brown and yellow plaid shirt, holding his right hand over his heart. And all around him were little bags of cement."

Cement? Did I hear that correctly?

"Cement. In the dream Jake never spoke. He just stood there very peacefully." Sue paused, then continued. "I've thought about it a lot. I believe that his hand over his heart means that he did not have pain. But what about the little bags of cement? I even looked up cement in a book on dream symbols, but of course, cement wasn't there. Then I had an idea: I wonder if Cement was another way of saying the word Emit. You know how dreams can scramble things and make symbols out of words."

When Sue said "Cement," I too had turned the word inside out and saw or heard "Emit." It made a peculiar kind of sense. At that moment another idea came to me. "Sue, the Hebrew word *Emet* means Truth."

I waited through a long silence at the other end of the phone. Then I heard Sue's small, quiet voice, almost a sob. "Oh Diane, how amazing. We have Time and Truth—our world, their world. Can you imagine what this means?"

The question was too big, too philosophical. The answer that came to me was very simple. "Maybe it means that Jake is taking good care of you. And Emit is truly a very special bear."

Sue's story folded into my psyche, and I felt a warm connection with Time and Truth, and with Sue and Jake and Dick. I slept very peacefully. And I imagined that Sue slept well too, with Emit curled up in her arms.

Two days after Christmas I called Sue. For a few minutes we talked about our holidays. A month before she had told me that she would travel to her hometown where all of her family and old friends live. "I'll be a part of everyone else's life—just there, not a part of anything." And that was exactly how it was. The holiday had been difficult for Sue. We both understood that feeling of being with others and feeling alone.

A moment later Sue's voice became upbeat. "Now I have to tell you something wonderful that happened. Across the street from my mother lives an older woman named Millie. She was our neighbor when I was growing up. She lost her husband when I was a little girl. She never had any children; she never remarried. She has always seemed so lonely to me. When Jake died, she came over to express her condolences, and I remember she said, 'I know how hard it's going to be.'"

Sue continued, "A few days before Christmas, I began thinking about Millie. I saw an ad for teddy bears. A local department store was donating money to the Make-A-Wish Foundation for every bear sold. All of a sudden, I had an idea: I would take a bear to Millie. Maybe a bear would give her the comfort and the company that Emit gives me. Then I thought, I hardly know this woman. We were never close. What will she think? I debated with myself, but I knew it was something I had to do. I told myself, 'You're going!' The day before Christmas, I went to the store and bought a cuddly bear and put it in a gift bag."

On Christmas day Sue crossed the street and rang Millie's doorbell. "There I stood, holding this big bag with a bear popping out. When Millie came to the door, she looked at me questioningly. When I told her I had a gift for her, I could see tiny tears in her eyes. We went inside. I gave her the bear and explained to her about Emit. Then I said, 'Maybe he could turn out to be your best friend, like Emit is for me.' Millie began to cry. Through her tears, she kept repeating, 'This is such a surprise! I am so surprised! No one has ever surprised me like this before!'"

The women sat down and talked. Millie wept quietly as she held the bear to her. She told Sue that in June she had lost her brother, the last of her nine siblings. This Christmas she was truly alone. Recently she had had an accident and been hurt. Who could she talk to? She was completely alone.

Sue said, "Now you will have an ear to hear these things."

As Sue was leaving, Millie asked, "What shall I name it?"

Sue replied, "This is your personal bear, and you are the one who should name it."

As she finished her story, I felt humbled by the absolute beauty of what Sue had done. When I told Sue what a *mitzvah*, a blessed deed, she had done, Sue replied. "All I know is that this was the best gift I could have given to myself, that I could do something to help someone else. I kept thinking about how you gave me Rabbi Grollman's book on grieving when Jake died. You told me then that even though I couldn't imagine it now, someday I would pass the book along to help someone else. I couldn't give Millie the book. That wasn't what she needed, but I could give her a bear. I really understand now that what you give is the excitement and the meaning of Christmas and of Chanukah. I could never have received a present that would make me feel this good."

Dear Sue, today you gave me two special gifts: a beautiful story of Christmas spirit, and the gladness in knowing that by reaching out with your own heart to someone else, you were finding your own way to heal.

Sue's healing may have been prolonged because she has been so alone in her journey. For many years Jake was her best friend. They enjoyed each other's company so much that they never felt a need to seek out a wider circle.

When Jake died, Sue's religious faith became a solace for her, and she attended Mass regularly. Yet she still felt isolated in her grief.

Because she was never blessed with children, Sue did not have the comfort of a son's strong arm or a daughter's warm hug. Sue's mother, her three siblings, their spouses, and her nieces and nephew were devoted to her and supported her in every way, but they lived two hours away. Visiting them involved a long, lonely, and exhausting drive for Sue. Sometimes when she returned home on Sunday evening, she felt even more alone.

Although Sue's many friends at work were sympathetic and supportive, they didn't always know what to do or say to help her. Once the workday was over, her co-workers went their own separate ways, back to their own busy lives.

Over the months I often told Sue about our Grief Group, how much it helped to talk and listen to other women who had suffered the same loss.

Sue said, "What I would have given in those first months to have even one woman friend who could understand what I was going through. I had no 'best girlfriend' that I could just melt down with. Except for an elderly lady, I knew no one who had lost her soulmate."

When people did reach out, Sue found it hard to accept their kindness. "In the early months a few dear friends reached out to me, but I was trapped in the loss of Jake. He was all I could focus on. I didn't have the strength to respond to people who wanted to help me."

Neighbors tried to include Sue in outings to hockey games or on shopping trips. "Knowing that someone was reaching out was some comfort, but I couldn't muster the energy to go. I would say, 'Thank you. I'm not ready. When I can, I'll take you up on it.'"

Between household chores, working full time, and grieving, Sue was drained. "I didn't have the steam to do one extra thing. It felt like I was in a comatose state. I was glad just to get through each day."

As the months passed, Sue realized that she was constantly anguishing over aspects of her life, that she was often anxious and fearful. One day she began writing in a little tablet what was troubling her. "Just setting my thoughts down on a piece of paper helped me put things in perspective. This has been so beneficial."

Sue has also turned to reading for guidance and support. "I purchase helpful little books and read a few pages each night. My favorite is *Don't Sweat the Small Stuff . . . and it's all small stuff* by Richard Carlson [6]. Every time I pick it up, it gives me a little lift.

"The other book I love to read is *Healing After Loss ~ Daily Meditations for Working Through Grief* by Martha Hickman [7]. The book has a passage for every day of the year, for day-by-day healing. It is a wonderful source for people who need to find enlightenment every day. The book reflects exactly how I feel. It keeps me tuned in to my feelings. At the beginning, it let me know that I was not crazy. Later it told me that I couldn't dwell on my grief, that I must go forward. I was able to visualize Jake in my mind's eye and know that he was still with me, supporting me on the difficult path I was traveling."

Six weeks before Jake died, Sue had major surgery. Over a year later, she developed some serious health problems. When Sue explained to her new specialist what she had been through, the doctor felt certain that a combination of her surgery and the shock of Jake's death had triggered her illness.

Sue told me, "I realize now that since Jake died, I have been functioning in shock. My body took the impact. It all caught up with me."

Toward the end of 2000, as she began to feel better physically, her energy level grew, and the weight of her world seemed lighter. On New Year's Day, Sue made some resolutions. "I realized that I needed to change my life. I decided that this year I would take the initiative to get involved and find some new activities that interest me. I need to be with people. If I'm around other people, I know I will make new friends."

She hesitated a moment, then continued. "You know, Diane, in some ways this time is even harder than the beginning. Trying to break out, to open up to a new life that's been thrown at you is scary. It's not glamorous or easy to develop a new life of your own."

One day in January, Sue saw that an ice show production of *Beauty and the Beast* was coming to a nearby town. "That story has always been one of my favorites. I really wanted to go, but I had no one to go with. I said to myself, 'Sue, you really want to go. You have two choices: you can stay home alone and feel sorry for yourself or you can buy a ticket and go.' And that's what I did. I went alone!"

Concerned that going alone could have been depressing, I asked, "How was it?"

Sue's voice danced through the telephone. "You know what? I enjoyed every minute of it! And I was so proud of myself!" We both celebrated her victory. Once again I marveled at Sue's courage.

Since Jake's death, Sue has had to be her own therapist, support group, and best friend. Over time she has come to understand very clearly what she needs in her life and how to achieve it. With her inner strength and new determination, she will move forward, at her own pace, in her own way, all in good time—her time.

CHAPTER 19

One More Good-Bye

In Judaism, a special ceremony dedicates the permanent headstone and marks the official end of mourning for Jews. When the mourners arrive at the cemetery, the stone is covered with a cloth. During the brief memorial service, called the unveiling or the stone dedication, the cloth is removed. The dedication can be held at any time, but usually it occurs within the first year.

I heard several explanations of the unveiling. One woman told me that mourning is a matter of degrees, and this marking of time is to remind the mourners that they have traversed many levels in the intensity of their grief; they have survived, and their mourning is now at a different level. A second reason given was that the dedication is a way to bring people back to the cemetery, for those who find the visit unbearable. After the dedication, they should be able to return more easily. A third explanation was that the unveiling underscores the reality of the death. A friend told me that she felt a great sense of relief when her husband's grave was marked by a permanent stone rather than a flimsy marker.

Some people spoke of the unveiling as a time for "closure," a term I found disturbing. To me it sounded like a mean thud, closing the book of someone's life, almost as though they had never existed. I came across a passage from the *Shulcan Aruch*, a 16th century code of Jewish law: "One should not grieve too much for the dead, and whoever grieves excessively is really grieving for someone else" [8]. Somewhere between stark "closure" and "excessive grief" lie the treasures of memory, a sadness that may never leave, and a love that may change but never end.

We planned the unveiling for the Friday after Thanksgiving, when many family members would be in town. As the time drew near, I felt some anxiety. The struggle had been great, but over the months I had gradually reentered life; my pain was less acute. I feared a ripping away of the protective layers that now separated me from January 24. Still, I felt certain that Judaism, in its wisdom, had a very good reason for this tradition, and when the time came, I would understand.

141

Although some dedications are open to friends, we decided that we would not make this a public event. None of us wanted to relive the funeral. Only immediate family would be there: Fred, Bruce and Margie, Karen and Leonard, and Dick's nieces Hallie and Jennifer, his nephews Jordy and Harlan; Dick's Uncle Ed. When I called the synagogue, I learned that the rabbi would not be available to conduct the service; however, because this is not a formal service, a rabbi is not necessary. Lay people can conduct the ceremony.

Even this hiccup in our plans was *b'shert*. When I told Fred, without any hesitation he said that he would like to prepare and conduct the service in memory of his father. He spent many hours and much thought in the planning, and this was especially meaningful for him. Several of us wrote our own sentiments, which we read at the service.

The day was clear and extremely cold. As our little group filed up the slight rise to the gravesite, our footsteps crunched across the starched, icy grass. We read the poems, the narratives, and the prayers. When Fred lifted the sheeting that covered the black headstone, which had been set in the ground earlier in the week, we recited the Mourners' *Kaddish*, the prayer in memory of the dead.

When the service was finished, Fred passed around a basket, and each of us took a seashell and a cigar to place on the gravestone. Dick would have wept proudly at the sentiments, smiled at the shells, and laughed at the cigars. And he would have felt great joy that the people he loved best were holding each other's hands as we remembered him in a unique and personal way. His family, and most especially his son, had paid him the greatest tribute, created in and permeated with love, admiration, and finally peacefulness of spirit. We knew that our service was the best way we could have honored Dick.

In the quiet intimacy of the day, we all wept, each with our own thoughts and memories of the ebullient man with whom we had each shared life and laughter, whom we all missed so much. But the tears were different from the last time we had gathered here on that cold January day. These were not the acid, acrid tears of shock, the tears that still denied, the tears that knew but did not yet believe. These were softer tears, from a place so deep that it cannot be named, tears of almost-acceptance, tears that know-believe that Dick will not come back to us, tears that know-believe that each of us will survive. We had learned that the circle of life does continue. Standing in the snow, I remembered that the *Kaddish*, which we had just recited, never refers to death, but rather it reminds us of the greatness of God. The opening words, *Yitgadal ve-yitkadash, Shmei rabbah,* mean "May His name be magnified and made holy." The *Kaddish*, and our dedication today, were affirmations of life.

Service for the Memorial Unveiling
Of Richard A. Kaimann
November 26, 1999

Fred:

O Great Spirit,
    whose voice I hear in the winds
    and whose breath gives life to all the world,
    hear me.
I am small and weak.
I need your strength and wisdom.
Let me walk in beauty
    and let my eyes ever behold the red and purple sunset.
Make my hands respect the things you have made
    and my ears grow sharp to hear your voice.
Make me wise so that I may understand the things
    you have taught my people.
Let me learn the lessons you have hidden
    in every leaf and rock.
Make me always ready
    to come to you with clean hands and straight eyes
So when life fades as the fading sunset
    my spirit may come to you without shame.

Great Spirit of the heavens,
    Lift me up to you
    That my heart may worship you
    And come to you in glory.
Hold in my memory that you are my Creator,
    Greater than I,
    Eager for my good life.
Let everything that is in the world
    Lift my mind,
    and my heart,
    and my life to you
    so that we may come always to you
        in truth and in heart.

From "Let Me Walk In Beauty" [9]

Hallie:

מִזְמוֹר לְדָוִד ה׳ רֹעִי לֹא אֶחְסָר:

בִּנְאוֹת דֶּשֶׁא יַרְבִּיצֵנִי עַל־מֵי מְנוּחוֹת יְנַהֲלֵנִי:

נַפְשִׁי יְשׁוֹבֵב יַנְחֵנִי בְמַעְגְּלֵי־צֶדֶק לְמַעַן שְׁמוֹ:

גַּם כִּי־אֵלֵךְ בְּגֵיא צַלְמָוֶת לֹא־אִירָא רָע כִּי־אַתָּה עִמָּדִי

שִׁבְטְךָ וּמִשְׁעַנְתֶּךָ הֵמָּה יְנַחֲמֻנִי:

תַּעֲרֹךְ לְפָנַי שֻׁלְחָן נֶגֶד צֹרְרָי דִּשַּׁנְתָּ בַשֶּׁמֶן רֹאשִׁי כּוֹסִי

רְוָיָה:

אַךְ טוֹב וָחֶסֶד יִרְדְּפוּנִי כָּל־יְמֵי חַיָּי וְשַׁבְתִּי בְּבֵית יְיָ

לְאֹרֶךְ יָמִים:

23rd Psalm

Harlan:

The Lord is my shepherd, I shall not want.
You make me lie down in green pastures,
You lead me beside still waters. You restore my soul.
You guide me in paths of righteousness for Your name's sake.
Yes, even when I walk through the valley of the shadow of death,
I will fear no evil, for You are with me;
With rod and staff You comfort me.
You prepare a table before me in the presence of my enemies;
You have anointed my head with oil; my cup overflows.
Surely, goodness and mercy shall follow me all the days of my life,
And I shall dwell in the house of the Eternal God forever.

Diane:

Missing You (from p. 3)

Karen:

The pain of that cold winter day almost a year ago was so intense that I didn't notice it until I heard Leonard mutter from behind me, "I can't stand that noise."

I looked around, wondered, "What noise?" He drew my attention to the heavy sound of rushing water coming from the gravesite. It was a grim sound, like an angry ocean rushing in, swirling, rushing again, over and over, insistent, rough, punishing. Once I was aware of it, it became too much to bear.

During these last months, as I have tried to come to terms with the sudden loss of a brother only recently found, the sound has softened somewhat. Now I can hear dolphins in it at times, gently urging Dick toward a more peaceful place, free of any worries.

The ocean was Dick's ally; he loved being in it. That ocean surrounded him when he left us. It surrounded him here where we stand now. It surrounds and soothes him for eternity.

Fred:

I wish to say something, if modest, meaningless and small. But I am no one. None of us are—just shadows of the divine, specks in the universe and a fraction of our own potential. Yet we struggle, silently, yellingly, self-importantly, anonymously, modestly, nobly and forgottenly.

But we struggle nonetheless. Such is the power of life. I never imagined that at 30, I would be a standard-bearer for my line. Where are the others? Where are the lions of my childhood? The vibrant parents, grandparents, great aunts and great uncles gnawing at life's sweet meat. I can still hear their roar. Why can't I luxuriate in the warmth of their thick coats or enjoy their ferocious protection?

So let me ponder the imponderable now, at a wayside as good as any. What is life? And who are we? Silly fool. This can't be asked, let alone answered. Can the swimmer struggling around the vortex of a sinking ship say what it means to be wet? Or the accountant under a tax-time typhoon of schedules, withholdings, deductions, and exemptions contemplate Zeno's paradoxes?

Here's a try anyway. There's a certain phrase quite popular lately: "It takes a village." Let me propose a variation: "We are a village." We are each a village ourselves. Each of us is the sum of our parts—our parents, family, friends, teachers, colleagues, and community—all mixing to greater or lesser degrees the values, memories, genes, and conditions they bequeath to shape our endless futures.

Just like Dick was the culmination, if only for a moment, of his predecessors, so too am I Dick. And I am Julie, my mother, and her parents Rita and Max, and Dick's parents, Benno and Rosalie, and so many others going back so far that no one alive today remembers their names.

And it comforts me to know that I am not alone, and never will be.

The memories of the past may fade, but they never die.

The stone is unveiled.

Jordy:

We consecrate this memorial to Richard Allen Kaimann as a sign of undying love.

May his soul be bound up in the bond of eternal life.

God of infinite love, in whose trust are the souls of all the living and in whose keeping are the spirits of all flesh, standing at the grave of Uncle Dick, we gratefully recall his goodness, and we give thanks for the solace of memory and the gradually shrinking burden that comes with the passage of time.

We pray for strength that, walking through the valley of the shadow of death, we may be guided by light eternal. May our actions and aspirations honor Uncle Dick's memory as surely as does this monument, which will stand as a symbol of our respect and memory. He will live on as a blessing among us.

Ed begins, all join: Mourners Kaddish

יִתְגַּדַּל וְיִתְקַדַּשׁ שְׁמֵהּ רַבָּא בְּעָלְמָא דִּי־בְרָא
כִרְעוּתֵהּ. וְיַמְלִיךְ מַלְכוּתֵהּ בְּחַיֵּיכוֹן וּבְיוֹמֵיכוֹן וּבְחַיֵּי
דְכָל בֵּית יִשְׂרָאֵל בַּעֲגָלָא וּבִזְמַן קָרִיב וְאִמְרוּ אָמֵן:

Congregation and Mourners

יְהֵא שְׁמֵהּ רַבָּא מְבָרַךְ לְעָלַם וּלְעָלְמֵי עָלְמַיָּא:

Mourners

יִתְבָּרַךְ וְיִשְׁתַּבַּח וְיִתְפָּאַר וְיִתְרוֹמַם וְיִתְנַשֵּׂא וְיִתְהַדָּר
וְיִתְעַלֶּה וְיִתְהַלָּל שְׁמֵהּ דְּקוּדְשָׁא בְּרִיךְ הוּא. לְעֵלָּא מִן־
כָּל־בִּרְכָתָא וְשִׁירָתָא תֻּשְׁבְּחָתָא וְנֶחֱמָתָא דַּאֲמִירָן
בְּעָלְמָא וְאִמְרוּ אָמֵן:

Mourners

יְהֵא שְׁלָמָא רַבָּא מִן שְׁמַיָּא וְחַיִּים עָלֵינוּ וְעַל כָּל
יִשְׂרָאֵל וְאִמְרוּ אָמֵן:

Mourners

עֹשֶׂה שָׁלוֹם בִּמְרוֹמָיו הוּא יַעֲשֶׂה שָׁלוֹם עָלֵינוּ וְעַל־
כָּל יִשְׂרָאֵל. וְאִמְרוּ אָמֵן:

Jennifer:

Let the glory of God be extolled, and God's great name be hallowed in the world whose creation God willed. May God rule in our own day, in our own lives, and in the life of all Israel, and let us say: *Amen.*

Let God's great name be blessed for ever and ever. Beyond all the praises, songs and adorations that we can utter is the Holy One, the Blessed One, whom yet we glorify, honor, and exalt. And let us say: *Amen.*

For us and for all Israel, may the blessing of peace and the promise of life come true, and let us say: *Amen.*

May the One who causes people to reign in the high heavens, let peace descend on us, on all Israel and all the world, and let us say: *Amen.*

ଔ ଔ ଔ

Dick's final gifts were the values he held most dear: love among family, respect and honor, integrity, and joy in life. No one loved life more than Dick. No one would be more emphatic that we end our mourning and *see more beauty.*

Standing in the snow, I began to understand this ancient ritual, on many levels.

CHAPTER 20

"Every Day is a Challenge"

At my first meeting of the Grief Group, a widow of five years looked at me compassionately and said, "Every day will be a challenge." Around the table, everyone nodded.

In the early phases of grief, many of our challenges were universal. We had to move through community customs and religious rituals surrounding death. At the same time, we were experiencing our own intense shock and grief. Because of the circumstances of Dick's death, I felt a compelling need to tell the story again and again. People would ask me questions. Depending on who the person was and how I was feeling at the time, I would give an abridged version or a very complete one. Either way, each retelling of the story reinforced the reality and brought some relief.

For all of us, too soon visitors were gone, back into their own lives. But what would we do with ours? How urgently we wanted to find some normalcy in a life turned upside down. When would we be ready to re-enter the world? Would we ever be? How do other people do this?

From reading and listening to friends, we learned that each person found her own pace and path for handling grief and re-entering life. Some women needed to be away from the house and even out of town, as much as possible. Home held too many memories. Other women cocooned themselves at home. Some forgot to eat, skipped meals, lost weight; others found comfort in food and ate too much.

Small tasks overwhelmed us. But we knew we needed to take care of ourselves; we had to venture out. We could not continue to rely on others. Each tiny step was a challenge. Before all the casseroles and cakes in the freezer were gone, we needed to purchase fresh fruit and vegetables. Several women could recall their first trip to the grocery store to buy food for which they had no taste. For one, pushing her shopping cart through the aisles felt like an out-of-body experience. This mundane chore had assumed cosmic proportions.

Our emotional reactions to ordinary parts of daily living would surprise us. Everything around us seemed so normal. How could the world go on, so unaltered, when our worlds were altered forever? It was incomprehensible. A week after the funeral, a friend invited me to a restaurant. This would be my first outing. Sitting at the table, I felt an invisible wall curl around me, separating me from everyone else. The carefree mood of the lunch crowd baffled me. Didn't they know that my husband had died? I tried to make normal conversation with my solicitous friend, but the effort was exhausting. I went home sadder than before.

No sooner was the funeral over than many of us had to face the complex business of death, dealing with estates, wills, banks, attorneys, and accountants.

In the fall of 1998, after two years of discussions between ourselves and with lawyers, Dick and I had finally found a trust attorney who was able to create the complicated estate plan that we wanted. We were leaving for Israel within days, and we agreed that the work must be complete. On November 6, 1998, we signed and sealed the final document.

Less than two months later, the lawyer and I were implementing that document. How fortuitous that we completed this work when we did. We had a clear, current document that expressed Dick's wishes. Without that, settling the estate would have been a nearly impossible task.

A few days after the funeral, I sat through a long, but necessary meeting that exhausted me. I must have signed my name a hundred times. As we grappled with all the deatils, sometimes my mind clicked into gear; at other times, my concentration was nil.

We had a clear, current document that expressed Dick's wishes. Without that, settling the estate would have been a monumental and nearly impossible task.

Several women had stories about automobile mishaps that occurred shortly after their husbands' death.

In mid-February, I was still feeling very shaky, but I invited my sister-in-law Karen out for her birthday lunch. We both looked forward to going to a quaint English tearoom in Waukesha, a town thirty miles away. On Friday morning, I picked up Karen, and we set out on our jaunt. When we exited the freeway, neither of us was sure how to find the restaurant, but we would drive around and find it. At a stop sign, I hesitated for a few extra seconds, and the man behind us rammed into the back of the car. No one was hurt, but the car—Dick's new car—would require major bodywork. The other driver was very kind and took full responsibility. My first thought was "How will I explain this to Dick?" I tried not to cry.

Seeing that I was badly shaken, Karen offered to drive us home, but I was determined to continue with our plans. To my surprise, I was able to drive. We easily found the restaurant and had a lovely lunch. We took the car to the shop for an estimate, did a few errands, and finally set out for home.

Because I had wanted to celebrate Karen's birthday in a special way, I had taken on more than I was ready to handle. We could have stayed closer to home and had a fine time. I was learning that, at least for now, I needed to respect my fragile state and my instincts.

I berated myself for being careless and inattentive. Then I thought, "What could you expect, at a time like this?" I felt terrible about the car. At last I decided that in the greater scheme of things, this event was not important. And it was, after all, just a car.

In May a friend suggested lunch and shopping. I couldn't fathom why I would want to buy anything. In a shop I spotted a denim suit that seemed nice. "It would be practical," I told myself. But buying it seemed disrespectful, vain, and self-indulgent. With encouragement from my friend, I reluctantly made the purchase. Carrying the shopping bag from the store, I felt awkward, but I told myself this was another step toward normalcy. When fall arrived, I was able to indulge my love of clothes without feeling guilty. I purchased a handsome brown leather jacket and considered it a gift I was giving myself; it felt good.

In so many ways, I felt vulnerable, thin-skinned. Peculiar things caused tiny needle pricks of pain. One day in March, I went to a new doctor and had to fill in the registration form. *Check one: Single ____ Married ____ Widowed ____* Wasn't I "All of the above"?

Person to notify in case of emergency _____

Were these probing questions designed to torture me, to remind me of my aloneness and my new status? I rushed through the form and picked up a magazine.

No one warned me about spring.

In January, February, March, when my street was silent, and my neighbors dashed between car and shelter, when the earth was white and frozen solid, and sunshine was a rarity, I could stay indoors like everyone else. Insulated by winter, I felt safe. I could contain my grief inside my house, inside my heart. Winter grieving had become a familiar way of life.

Why did spring sting so badly? I had wished desperately for time to pass, but I hadn't anticipated how difficult the change of seasons would be. Suddenly, I didn't want to let go of winter, the last season Dick and I had shared, the last season he had known. As much as I had always feared and dreaded our Wisconsin winters, this year I didn't want winter to end.

In March no buds had appeared yet, no green blades of grass, but the calendar and letters from lawn services bore down upon me like an avalanche. Too soon April arrived. Walkers and bikers appeared on the streets; children shed parkas and boots and ran out to play, energized by warm air and more hours of daylight. In the grocery store, I overheard tidbits of conversation—families planning gardens, picnics, long walks, bike rides, cookouts, vacations. What would I do with spring and summer? Blank. All I could foresee was Blank.

When my children were born, I had looked forward to each change of season. "This will be the baby's first spring—his first summer, her first fall." Now I could only think, "Dick will miss spring and summer. This will be my first spring alone, my first summer without my husband." The coin of my life had just turned upside down.

For this mourner, April was the cruelest month.

Everyone in the Grief Group agreed that the Jewish holidays were very difficult, particularly in the first year. The first holiday for me was Passover. My brother and sister-in-law invited me to fly down to Virginia to be with them. Margie couldn't take more time off from work, so I would have to go alone. Was it difficult? Yes. Barely three months had passed. Would it have been harder to stay at home? Probably. I could have invited myself to homes of friends, but going to Virginia was the right choice. Although I had a major meltdown during the day, in the evening I was able to participate in the service. What was important was that I was with my family.

Rosh Hashanah, the Jewish New Year, and Yom Kippur, the Day of Atonement, come in the fall. For the last twelve years Dick and I had gone to services together, sat in the same seats near the front, often held hands, kissed each other Happy New Year, and enjoyed being there together. How I dreaded this season. Couldn't we cancel the holidays, just this once?

Every year my friend Nancy invited us to Rosh Hashanah dinner. This year she prepared an entirely different menu; we ate in her dinette instead of in the dining room. With exquisite sensitivity, Nancy changed as many elements as possible, and that helped immensely. At Temple, I requested that we sit in the very last row. Perhaps the distance from the pulpit protected me. I had only a few teary moments.

On Saturday, Rosh Hashanah Day, I chose to stay home to read and think. In the early evening I remembered that last summer we had hosted a large picnic for Dick's cardiac rehab group. Someone had brought a camcorder and given us the tape. I had not forgotten about that, but I had not had the courage to watch it. I placed the tape in the VCR and turned on the TV. And there was Dick in his t-shirt and denim shorts, perched on his tractor lawn mower and pulling a large cart filled with supplies. He was puffing on his cigar and grinning his impish grin, the Lord of the Manor. Relaxed and happy, he was doing what he loved best, entertaining friends in his home. On the screen, he laughed as he roasted the bratwursts on the grill, served up the potato salad, and set out the gooey un-heart-healthy desserts prepared by the guests.

Amid the clamor of the picnic, I heard Dick speak only one sentence. I played and replayed those few seconds, just to hear his voice. That afternoon I had a long, cleansing cry. I put the video back into its case and prepared my dinner. Maybe I would watch the video again next year. Maybe I would need to cry that hard again. Maybe not.

Yom Kippur, a sad day by its very nature, presented a greater challenge. In late August, my stepson Fred had invited me to visit him for Yom Kippur. My first response was, "I'm still tired from Israel." Two minutes later I knew that I would go to New Jersey to be with Fred.

Several years ago, Fred lost his mom. Now his stepfather and I are the only parents he has. As we spoke, I realized how relieved and pleased I was with the invitation. I sensed that Fred needed me as much as I needed him.

It was a good decision. Being in a different synagogue, among strangers, with no visual image of Dick sitting there, insulated me. I did not have to face more condolences and mournful, pitying faces. Here I was anonymous. And Fred did not have to sit alone.

After the morning service on Yom Kippur Day, Fred was on a panel discussion with five other people, all at least twenty years his senior, who spoke about the meaning of Judaism in their lives. Because they would not be going home for lunch on this day of fasting, a large crowd attended the session. Fred was handsome, personable, and eloquent. How I hoped Dick's spirit was in that room!

After the talks a dozen people came up to congratulate Fred and welcome him to the congregation. At last I had my turn. Putting my arms around my stepson, I said quietly, "I am so proud of you. I wouldn't have missed this for the world. Your Dad would have been thrilled." Our eyes filled with tears.

It was a long day of praying and fasting, but mercifully the memorial service was brief. When it was over, Fred and I hugged again. "We made it," I said.

"We made it together."

What could have been a weekend of misery for both of us was a special time. Being together at Yom Kippur brought us to a new level of honesty and closeness. We needed each other; we shared our memories and our sorrow. We had done a *mitzvah*, a blessed deed, for each other.

Learning to live alone was a challenge for all of us. Most of us had suffered other losses. When my mother died, at a young 51, I was broken-hearted. But the core of my life was not ripped away. I had a husband and a child. When my dad died at age 84, I was again stricken with grief—and yet I had my husband to support me, and our daily lives didn't change.

When our husbands died, we were completely and utterly alone in our homes. We wandered through the empty rooms. We had never heard so much silence. We played music, kept on the television—sometimes all night—to keep us company, or to keep us sane, or just to stay connected with the outside world. Each evening we were keenly aware of how much we missed having someone to eat with, to chat about our day and discuss the news.

Perhaps that was why many of us turned to our new sisterhood for daily contact and for sharing our lives. Our children had their own grief to deal with, and we didn't want to weigh them down with our concerns, which were so different from theirs. When our children were involved in their own families and careers, lived far away, or were just not interested in the day-to-day tracking of our lives, we needed our women friends. They became the warp and woof of our new existence.

When we were no longer part of a couple, some of our married friends seemed to feel awkward or uncertain about whether to include us in their social lives. While acknowledging the loyalty of many married friends, some women were hurt when a few of those couples disappeared. We asked ourselves whether in our own safe, married lives we had gone out of our way to include single women. We recognized that deep empathy often comes only with personal experience.

Because of what we had all been through, and our new life structure, we now had more in common with our single women friends and we sought out those relationships. As our friendships strengthened, we came to treasure each one of them. Without them the journey would have been longer, lonelier, and far more difficult.

The network of women helped us to redefine our social world. My dinner for ten was more than food and good company. It was a sea change, a shift from the couples' world into the singles' world. My life now, and perhaps forever, would revolve around my women friends, and I wanted to participate actively.

Fortunately in this day and age in our society, women can go together to dinner and a movie, or travel together, without being self-conscious or uncomfortable. As single women, we learned to buy season tickets with friends for theater, ballet, opera, and symphony. We arranged social time with people whose company we enjoyed and whose interests we shared. We planned trips to Chicago for shows, shopping, and sightseeing. We filled in our calendars—eventually complaining that we were too busy! What had begun as filling time to protect ourselves from boredom and loneliness eventually became times we looked forward to. We made plans because the company and the event would be fun. We were running toward life, not away from it.

Even in the early stages, we looked for activities and projects to occupy and challenge us. In early February, my dear friend Lynn drove up from Chicago to visit. For 35 years she has been my mentor in fashion and decorating. Standing at my tiny desk in a dark, chilly back bedroom, she said, "If it were me, the first thing I would do is move into Dick's office. Then I would make this room into a beautiful guest room!"

Why does it take another set of caring eyes to point out the obvious?

"Will you help me?"

"Of course!"

This vigorous redecorating symbolized a new independence. Planning the guest room was fun. I selected paint and carpeting, put airy blinds on the window, and refinished an old desk. I planned a special trip to Chicago to shop with Lynn for the all-important down comforter, pillows, and linens. We placed a large peace lily near the window. Thinking of future guests, I purchased a small TV. One day in a consignment shop, I stumbled across a padded headboard for $10. Perfect! Done in shades of cream and green, the room is bright, warm, and inviting. Lynn's idea was an inspired gift that brought me joy at a joyless time in my life. Every time I pass by the doorway and look in, I feel uplifted.

When Hannah told me about redecorating her den, I chuckled. We had taken the same route to sanity by doing what we had always enjoyed. I recently found a newspaper article with the headline, "Widow Redecorates, Sets up Guest Room." There really is nothing new under the sun. Hannah and I had enjoyed designing our rooms and selecting colors, fabrics, and furnishings. Of course, it had felt strange to make all these decisions alone. Whom did we ask for approval? Only ourselves.

We especially enjoyed the physical labor: scraping and sanding, priming and painting the desks, while listening to the radio in our garages. We were surprised that those hours passed more quickly than most. We were sweating, we were accomplishing, and we were working with a tangible goal in mind. We felt proud of our ability to plan and complete a project by ourselves. Although we knew we could do it, we needed to prove it to ourselves. We were both delighted with the results, rooms that were entirely to our liking. What a feel-good!

An added benefit was a practical one. With all the mountains of paperwork in my new life, the new office made my work easier. Because Dick had worked from home, his spacious, sunny office contained a computer, fax machine, copy machine, file cabinets, shelves, and storage space. At first, I felt as though I was invading his space. Soon I found that being in the room where he had spent so much of his time helped me feel connected to him.

For many months, large maintenance projects kept me very busy. The house required interior and exterior painting, new gutters, and roof repairs. Cleaning out the basement was an endless task. Each project required time and planning: finding and selecting workmen, deciding whom to hire, negotiating price, and supervising work. It felt strange, sometimes overwhelming, to be responsible for every decision. I missed Dick's logical approach, his knowledge of household matters, his fiscal common sense. With each decision, I anguished as I tried to figure out what Dick would have wanted me to do. Ultimately, I decided that I would do what made sense and pleased me. I was learning to trust my own instincts and judgment in many new arenas. Once the decisions were made and the projects in motion, I sometimes had a heady feeling—I did it, and I did it myself!

In the back of my mind was the possibility that one day I would wake up and the house would be too big for me and too much to maintain. At least the major work would be completed, the house updated, and after one huge garage sale, I could be ready to sell the house. I knew I would thank myself later for doing all this work now. My preoccupation with these projects helped the hours and days pass. Even in February and March, the house kept me involved in life.

For a while it seemed that every day I had to deal with another practical problem that Dick would have handled. A lady bug infestation, a tree struck by lightning, a wasp's nest, a dead car battery, income taxes, visiting mice—these were my problems and mine alone. I learned to distinguish between what I could handle alone and what required outside assistance. If I didn't take care of these problems, no one would. Just when I thought I couldn't handle one more domestic crisis, I did.

My network of new friends, other women alone, provided an unexpected and excellent resource. A phone call or two would tell me where to find a reliable gutter man, a competent accountant, and the best auto body repair shop. Because I couldn't turn to my husband to find the answers, I called upon friends who had done their own research and were happy to share. Soon I discovered that I too had information to exchange. Like it or not, I was handling my life and nothing fell apart.

Surprisingly, routine household tasks took on emotional overtones. In the past, chores that I had done were for us. Now here I was, doing all this work only for me. When spring came and the snow melted, my yard reappeared. Did I have the energy or desire to do gardening this year? Did I really care whether I had flowers in the yard and on the front porch?

Sue expressed what I was feeling. "Things that I did automatically in the past now take much more effort. Even little things are such a job. My spirit to do them is diminished, and chores are a burden. Grieving robs such energy from you. Everything is a chore."

Even though I didn't really care much, I put on my clogs and garden gloves and set to work. My geraniums had their finest year.

Fall arrived, with all the winterizing that Wisconsin demands. Dick had always made this a major project, guy-stuff, and would allot an entire weekend for this work, which he loved to do. Now I was on my own, and I dreaded what loomed over me as yet another unwanted responsibility.

I decided I was tired of asking or paying for help. In mid-October, on a warm, sunny day, at about 3 o'clock, with an unexpected burst of energy, I put on my oldest jeans and sweatshirt. With determination in my heart I marched out the door. *I can do this.*

By 4:15, I had replaced the two screen doors with storm doors, reeled in the hoses and dragged them into the garage, loaded all the clay pots onto the wheelbarrow and driven them into the garage, pushed the heavy gas grill from the side patio into the garage, and lugged the patio lounge, four chairs, table, umbrella, and stand down to the basement.

I was sweaty and happy. That fall afternoon I learned that I could roll up my sleeves and say, "No big deal."

What do women do with their engagement and wedding rings? Some put them in the safe right away. Others wear them for years. Sara told me that she never even considered not wearing her wedding ring. Two years after Sidney's death, a friend asked her, "Why are you still wearing your ring?"

She moved it to her right hand. Seven years later, when she noticed a crack in the band, she placed the ring in her safety-deposit box, to save as an heirloom.

Some wives designed new rings using the stones, the gold, or both. One day I met a woman who was wearing a beautiful pendant on a necklace. When I admired it, she beamed, "These were our wedding rings. I wanted to have them with me all the time, so I had the two intertwined. I love wearing it. It makes me so happy."

For months I searched for my wedding ring in every conceivable place. It never turned up. Most likely I had scooped it up with some tissues and tossed it away. After six months I felt certain that it was lost. I filed a claim, received a check from the insurance company, and selected a wide gold band with several pavé diamonds. It could be or not be a wedding band. I chose it because I thought Dick would have liked its clean lines and simplicity. I wore it on my wedding ring finger because I felt naked without a ring there. Although I missed the ring Dick had given me, wearing the replacement ring gave me a modicum of peace.

What of our husbands' clothing? All the women described the difficulty of this sad but necessary process. Some women couldn't bear seeing their husbands' clothes and disposed of them immediately. Others kept the clothes for a year or more. The creative woman who so lovingly designed the pendant commissioned an Amish woman to make a quilt of her husband's ties, using the wedding ring pattern. As with so many decisions, we all did what felt right for us.

At the time of the funeral, Dick's two nephews, his son, and my brother were pleased to receive sweaters, jackets, ties, and the few pieces of jewelry. Even our nieces and my daughter were pleased to have some Packers gear, sweatshirts, and sweaters. This early phase of the process was surprisingly easy because I knew Dick would have been pleased. I saved several sweaters and shirts for myself, and for months I wore them because they gave me a warm feeling.

Going through our husbands' closets and drawers was gut-wrenching for all of us. Deciding what to do with everything was so vexing for me that for months I avoided decisions about the remaining clothes. At times I gave articles to friends who helped me along the way. Watching other men try on Dick's clothes, so recently acquired or worn, was heartbreaking. Who was this stranger wearing Dick's favorite camel hair blazer and the black wool pants? Who was that in Dick's favorite suit? I tried to be detached. Then I caught myself thinking, "Dick will really be upset that I'm giving away his clothes." Finally, it became so painful that I left the room and let the men take what they wanted.

Two of Dick's friends wore his shoe size. They each took a few pairs. A month later, I donated the rest to charity. As I dropped six pairs of fine, highly polished leather shoes of many hues into brown grocery bags, I had an existential meltdown. So this is where it all leads. Those shoes had so many miles left in them. Sobbing quietly, I placed the bags on the front porch for the pick-up and hurriedly closed the door.

For several more months, my out-of-season clothes shared half a closet with Dick's suits, jackets, and slacks. I couldn't part with them yet. I needed to look at them every now and then, to touch the scratchy or smooth wools, and to look again at the preppy jackets and the business suits that he took such pride in. One day I woke up and decided that I could use the closet space. I cried a little as I moved the remaining clothes into the guest room closet, out of my daily sight. I still couldn't let go. Two more months passed before I neatly packed up all of the remaining clothes and donated them.

I gave Dick's watch to Fred, and placed his wallet, travel case, glasses, and a few other items in a dresser drawer. Sometimes I heard my mind's voice saying, "When Dick comes back, he'll want everything just the way it was." Then I would blink my way back to reality.

When I met with each of the women, we rarely touched upon the subject of meeting men and going out. Our focus was on the grieving process. As time passed, I wondered how they felt about moving on in this area of their lives. Even considering the possibility of a new relationship is a quantum leap for a woman who has lost her husband. It implies an acceptance of her loss, possibly surmounting feelings of disloyalty, an ability to put the past in its own special place in her heart, and a willingness to consider a new and different future for herself. I discovered that, as with every other aspect of this journey, each person makes individual choices and moves at her own pace. At social gatherings with peers, I listened to discussions about men.

From newer widows I heard, "It's just too soon. I can't even think about that yet. I'll know when I'm ready." Then they would add wistfully, "Still, some male companionship—dinner, a movie—would be very nice."

The thought of "dating" can be frightening to someone who was married to the same person for thirty or forty years. One friend said that a cousin wanted to introduce her to a nice man. "I felt like a teenager. What would I say to him? I became so scared thinking about it that I told my friend to hold off. "

A poised, charming lady told me how nervous she was the first time she went out. "I actually said to the guy, 'I haven't been out on a date in thirty years, and I am really nervous!'"

The man smiled and said, "Me either—and me too!" They both relaxed.

Recently I met an attractive, articulate woman named Jean who has been alone for ten years. One evening we went out for dinner. I asked this veteran for her insights.

"This is such an individual matter, and women run the gamut on this one. I know some women who were eager to 'meet someone' right away. I was too numb, too sad, and too busy to think about a man. Some women find their lives very full and fulfilling without a man. Others simply don't want the responsibility."

Jean brought up the statistical realities. "Of course, with the overwhelming number of single women versus single men in our age group, it is difficult to meet appropriate men—especially if you're picky, like me!"

She continued, "What has been most important to me is a balanced life for myself—friends, work, music, classes, theater, travel. I was determined to build a full life as a woman alone. And I succeeded in doing that. I enjoy my women friends and I enjoy my life as a single woman. Over the years I have gone out with a number of men and that was fine. I certainly enjoy male company and conversation."

Was Jean interested in "meeting someone"?

Thoughtfully she said, "You know, I would like to, maybe not for marriage but for companionship, to share things with."

Then she mused, "Like everything else in this life, if it's meant to be, it will be." Then, with a twinkle in her eye, she added, "Meanwhile, I'm going to enjoy my life and make it the best that it can be."

The challenges never end. Because our lives go on, we have many moments when our spirits are lifted, when we are mighty glad to be alive. And still, years later, those moments are often bittersweet because our partners are not here to share them. The most joyous family occasion can plunge us back into sadness. Sometimes, without warning, strong emotions surge up all over again.

One day on an airplane I met Stacy, a woman from Detroit who had been alone for four years. As women do, we spoke about our lives.

She told me, "At the beginning I was determined to immerse myself in numerous activities in order to return to a sense of normalcy. The second Christmas after my husband died, I had a siege of depression that nearly laid me low. I had read about this 'grief attack' that could come unexpectedly two or even three years later. The realization of my aloneness sank in, especially the permanence of the situation. I was struck with the keen awareness that this is the way it is and the way it may always be. That holiday season was very hard for me."

In a quiet, sad voice, Stacy mused, "Losing my spouse, my dreams, our life together left a tremendous void. With that acknowledgment comes sorrow. Of course I am stronger now and have greater understanding. I know that I am moving through yet another phase of the grieving process."

Neither of us spoke for a few minutes. Then with a complete change of tone, Stacy turned to me and said, "You know, the next time I'm on an airplane, I'll be with my grandson. We're going to Disney World this spring!"

I smiled back. She was fine, and that told me that through all my own phases, I would be too.

At the beginning, normal situations and practical problems overwhelmed us. Concerns shared in the past were now ours alone. Every problem seemed formidable. Eventually the formidable became manageable; we made decisions more easily, anguished less, and turned to appropriate people for advice. No longer was every minor event cause for distress. Gradually we removed emotional trappings from non-emotional issues. We became self-reliant. We developed resourcefulness, stamina, and determination to cope with each situation.

The woman in the Grief Group was right—every day is a challenge—but with time, support, and practice, we learned to meet our challenges with courage and confidence.

CHAPTER 21

Common Threads

As the chapters of this book unfolded, I often stepped back and reflected upon the hardest questions.

How do women alone survive? What fuels our return to Life? What enables each of us to move forward, to tackle the obstacles, physical and emotional, and create a good life for ourselves? How have my friends and I not only survived but emerged stronger, more independent, with greater self-esteem and self-confidence? Where does strength come from? Where does comfort come from?

Time has passed and each of us has woven the design that is our new life. Always a work in progress, we have constantly blended new colors and interwoven new fibers, to see if they strengthen and enrich the texture. Each of us has accepted, rejected, unraveled, and stitched together our own unique patterns.

FAITH

The most essential thread that held us together was faith. Those for whom God was a constant and familiar presence found a solace and a source of strength upon which to draw, particularly in the first brutal hours and days. For those with the greatest faith, the early hours were more bearable. For some, our pain brought with it deeper spirituality and a need to return to God.

All of the women I spoke with found consolation in their faith, whether it was highly personal or within a religious setting. Some experienced great comfort at church or synagogue. The quiet, the peace, the safety, and the familiar words and music eased our pain and gave us strength to go on.

Embedded within our suffering, however, were many conflicting layers of emotions: love, hurt, frustration, and helplessness. Some heard our own voices cry out, "It's not fair. How could you do this to me?" Implied within our grief was anger at being left behind with all the responsibilities of carrying on. Our feelings were tangled and difficult to sort out. With pain of that magnitude, where else does one go but to God?

Prayer has been a part of my life. Often I express gratitude to God or seek His help in difficult times. We have a working relationship: I do the work, while God supports me with subtle gifts. When Dick died, a special sense of spirituality provided the comfort and strength I needed to survive. From the moment I met Paulette, I entered a new world, the world of spirit. Especially at the beginning, I felt Dick's presence keenly, as though he was not ready to leave me and was trying desperately to communicate with me in different ways. I welcomed every sign, every word.

Perhaps when all the trappings of life are stripped away by a death, our spiritual sensitivities are heightened. It is as though an antenna that was never connected is suddenly receiving at full force. Then and now I choose to believe that my dear husband, who was so determined and single-minded in life, found a way to reach me.

When my world disintegrated on that Sunday afternoon, I was ripped apart. It was this gaping wound in my soul that admitted me to a new spiritual and mystical world beyond anything I could ever have imagined. I had questions and Paulette gave me a pathway to answers. I allowed myself to accept this new experience, to transcend our separation. It was that or nothingness. Believing brought me so much more peace than logic or questioning.

It was the impact of Dick's death that changed my perception of the spirit world, divine intervention, and forces outside of ourselves that shape our lives. Because of what happened to me, I will always believe that the convergence of the right time, the right place, and the right people is not accidental.

I hope I will always be open to noticing and acknowledging miracles. If I am wrong, then no harm is done, and I have found some peace in the worst times. If I am right, then Dick is somewhere right now, smiling.

The other women's faith in the unseen remained strong. Hannah's absolute faith has carried her through her worst times. Eliana believes that Elliott visited her friend. Jake's spirit comes to Sue through Emit the bear. All of us experienced some spiritual connection, feeling the presence of our partners, hearing their voices in our heads, talking to them and believing that somehow they could hear—all these moments brought comfort and the fragile edges of peace.

SUDDEN DEATH / PROLONGED ILLNESS

For the surviving spouse, the impact of death after a long, dreadful illness is quite unlike the impact of a sudden, unexpected death. Despite our many shared experiences and feelings after a loss, initially differences did exist.

Because our partners died suddenly, Sue, Sara, our families, and I were spared a prolonged illness, struggle, and suffering. We did not carry around double sets of images in our minds, the healthy man and the sick one, but we did have one indelible, enduring image: the events of that day—where we were, what we did, how we heard, what was said. The images played over and over in our mind's eye for a long time. Gradually, the pictures began to fade as our lives filled up again, and we were grateful.

On the other hand, many of the women suffered months or years of fatiguing, difficult care-taking and heartbreaking dedication as they watched their husbands dying day by agonizing day. When their men died, the women were physically, emotionally, and spiritually exhausted. Living grief had already drained them. Shari told me that her grieving began on the day of Rex's diagnosis.

Because Dick and I never had time to say "Good-bye," I wondered if couples who had the time told each other what was in their hearts. I wondered if they took the opportunity to talk about what their life together meant to them, and to consider what might happen afterwards. Did they say, "I love you more than life itself. I will miss you every day of my life. You have been my best friend. Thank you for you and for us. Good-bye, my dearest one."

Many women said that they experienced a special closeness during their husbands' illnesses, but that for the most part they shunned talking about death, fear, spiritual beliefs, and even plans for the wife's future. Confronting such topics would have undermined the atmosphere of cheerfulness, encouragement, and hopefulness that each woman tried to maintain. It would have admitted the unimaginable. By the time death was imminent, the men were often too weak and too ill for deep or serious discussions.

Most of my friends whose husbands were ill knew what lay ahead; yet, when death came, they were stunned by what was still sudden, shocking, incredible. In the earliest stages, the shock of death, the denial, the disbelief differed little among us. No matter how long the illness or how sudden the death, it took time for the reality to sink in, and even that reality was in and out of focus for a long time. Day after day, flashes of memory made us shake our heads as we tried again and again to absorb the fact of death. In the end, all of us were alone. We asked the universe, "How can the world continue without this man, my other half? How can I go on?"

After the initial shock, we all stumbled insensate through the dreadful early days and weeks, accepting the phone calls and visitors. We were worn out. We desperately needed sleep, and that was often elusive, erratic, and not refreshing. Most of us wept intermittently, wailing, calling out our questions and our pain to the silent walls.

Sometimes we heard our minds saying, "Soon he will come home from his trip. He'll sit down to dinner and ask what all the fuss is about."

Sudden or anticipated, death is death.

UNANSWERED QUESTIONS

Living with unanswered questions can plague a survivor. When a death is sudden, we lose even the opportunity to ask about subjects that we had perhaps avoided—or simply ignored when caught up in daily existence. At times I found myself wondering who Dick really was, trying to capture the essence of this man. When someone dies, his is a completed story. Now we have time to ponder that life.

At times I was curious. "Who was your favorite author? Composer? What was your favorite sport? Your favorite season? Your favorite food?"

Sometimes more pressing questions surfaced, "Were you satisfied with your accomplishments? Are you glad you chose your field of work? What were you most proud of? Did you have enough fun? Were there loose ends—friends forgotten, books unread, fences unmended—that you left behind? What would you do differently? How would you want to be remembered?"

Closer to the bone, I wondered, "Was I a good wife?"

How odd that now that he was gone, I longed to know my husband better. But I have learned to live with ambiguity.

In the Jewish tradition, people often write what is called an Ethical Will. This frequently takes the form of a letter to one's family. A few months after Dick's death, because I was struggling with lingering questions, I decided to create my own Ethical Will.

One Sunday afternoon I sat down and wrote long letters to my children, expressing all the sentiments I have trouble saying aloud to them: my pride in them, my overpowering love for them, my hopes for their futures. I also set down some of my ideas about what I consider important, values I hold dear. I asked forgiveness for the ways I might have hurt or failed them. Even though I cried, writing the letters was important for me. My two sealed envelopes are in a small safe, waiting. If I should die suddenly or be unable to express myself at the end, I hope that my children will never wonder who their mother really was or how much she loved them.

How I wish Dick had written such letters to Fred, to Karen, and to me. How I wish Jake had written such letters to Bruce, Margie, and to Sue.

FAMILY AND FRIENDS

From those early hours in Hawaii, strangers, then family and friends, have been my strongest support. For the five days before and after the funeral, the house was filled with people offering hugs, consolation, and quiet conversation.

It is often difficult for people to know what to do and say when they first see a friend who has lost a spouse. Do we hug her? Say "I'm so sorry"? Talk about her husband? Recall our own memories of him? Invite her to lunch or dinner?

Talk about our families and ourselves? Offer to go to the grocery store? Let her cry?

From my experience, the answer to all these questions can be "Yes," but we need to be gentle and take the lead from the mourner. Until we see a friend's face or hear her voice, we don't know if this is a good day or a bad one, a better moment or a terrible one. A quiet voice, a touch, and a listening ear are the best offerings.

Long after the last condolence call, our families have been our continuing support. Every woman expressed deep appreciation for her family. The love and tender attentions of caring children, parents, siblings, in-laws, nieces, nephews, extended family, and grandchildren have kept us going. They have held us up, nurtured us, and encouraged us.

Grandchildren in particular are a joyful and revitalizing thread for the women who are so blessed. It is hard to be sad in the presence of energetic youngsters. Naomi sees her beloved Nathan in Adam, as he climbs into his grandfather's chair on Passover. Another friend announces the pregnancy of her daughter-in-law and every line of sadness falls away, leaving the untroubled, radiant face of a woman half her age.

Our families and friends have been the bedrock of our survival and our healing, and for that we will always be grateful.

COMMUNITY

As time passed, many women found support in community.

A vital lifeline for many of us was the synagogue Grief Group. Every woman in our group expressed how much it helped to have a safe place where she could speak freely of her sorrow. Friends and even family may have been discomfited by conversations about our deceased husbands, but we desperately needed to talk about them, to feel connected through some anecdote or recollection.

In the first few weeks, the Grief Group became a destination for me, a scheduled activity that was designed to do what I needed: provide respite and a forum to talk about my grief with people who would understand. The most I could handle was dressing myself and going to the synagogue. I could drive there and back without having to hide my long face from outsiders. I needed no challenges, like having to smile at a stranger when I wanted to cry. I only traveled on city streets, avoiding the freeway. The speeding cars and trucks were too much for me. They reflected a level of energy I did not have.

Our Grief Group was fortunate to have Rabbi Silberg, a man who brought not only his own compassion, but also the wisdom of our tradition. I always came away with something to hold onto. At my very first meeting, about six weeks after Dick's death, the rabbi commented that in the first days and weeks, whatever we do in our lives seems like "just so much fodder." That was exactly how my life felt in February, March, and April—fodder. I was going through the motions of living, marking time. A few months later, that feeling was gone and what I had considered fodder was real life, the routine acts and activities that comprise our lives.

Sitting in the rabbi's study—a calm, uncluttered, sheltering room with a large, lovely palm—we could pour out our personal feelings. We could test our amalgam of emotions—loneliness, anger, resentment, fear, inadequacy, invisibility, and immobility—before a sympathetic sounding board. What a relief it was to hear that other women had exactly the same feelings. What a help to hear how they lived with and through their own turbulent times. We all listened to the others and learned. Several of the "veterans" told me that it felt good to be able to offer support and suggestions to newcomers. They became aware of their own progress, and this was another step in their healing.

Sara, who works full time and was unable to attend, told me she envied those of us who were able to participate in the Grief Group. "It is crucial to have other widows to talk to about grieving," Sara said. "I know I would have healed more quickly and more easily if I had had that support."

A number of women sought out counseling and found that speaking with a professional allowed them to express their feelings and gave them new insights and perspectives on their lives. The encouragement and feedback of a compassionate and skilled therapist were extremely valuable.

READING

Although I have met a few women who refused to read anything about grieving—it was all too familiar—most of us turned to books for comfort, insight, and inspiration. Books on grieving became our new loving companions.

Of the many books I read, one long remained on my night table. I read and reread *Living When A Loved One Has Died* by Earl A. Grollman [10]. Its tender wisdom was a balm for my soul. Later I found a wonderful friend in *To Begin Again* by Naomi Levy [11]. Both these books brought solace and the welcome assurance that my feelings, actions, fears, and moods were normal and typical. They also offered a glimmer that someday life would be better.

Although my concentration was limited at first, I was determined to keep up with my book club. This was a part of my life separate from Dick, a very satisfying part, and I didn't want to lose it. At the February meeting, I was amazed that I could participate. In May, my sister-in-law Karen and I led a discussion on *Sacred Hunger,* a long and complex book about a slave ship in the 1600s [12]. We did a respectable job. I wondered what the other members were thinking, as they observed the surviving sister and spouse dig into the history of slavery. To this day, I don't know how we did it.

NATURE AND BEAUTY

For some, the wonders of nature have become the connection to spirit.

A double rainbow appears when Doug's ashes are scattered over the river, and on the same day, his daughter looks up and sees a sparkling rainbow above. Shari and her family plant a tree to honor Rex, and just at that moment a rainbow drapes the sky. Coincidences?

Hannah and Ramona grow spectacular indoor and outdoor plants, lovingly planned and tended, reminding them of the beauty of this world and the cycle of life and rebirth in nature.

For others a love of beauty continues to be sustaining. Ramona's antiques and paintings are a constant source of joy and renewal for her. Shari's artwork brightens her life and reminds her daily of the sparkle in the life she and Rex shared. Eliana's imaginative, colorful artwork lifts her spirits.

In nearly every home I visited, classical music, opera, even jazz, played continuously, permeating the house with a special richness and tranquility. For so many, music is a perpetual source of pleasure and sustenance.

"Music hath charms to soothe the savage breast, To soften rocks, or bend a knotted oak." This familiar line comes from a play written in 1697 by William Congreve. Ironically, the name of the play is *The Mourning Bride.*

LEARNING AND CLASSES

Classes fill time, teach skills or expand knowledge, and engage the mind. Over time most of the women enrolled in some kind of continuing education courses, in local colleges and museums, in churches or synagogues. Some took lessons in bridge or golf, creating another outlet for socialization. Several took seminars in investment and financial management.

Many of my peers became computer-competent. Women who had wrestled with programming the VCR took classes to learn how to use the Internet, send e-mails, do research, write letters, and maintain financial records. They were keeping up with the world, an important component in staying young. It is invigorating to hear my friends discussing uploading, downloading, RAM, high-speed Internet, spreadsheets, scanners, links, wallpaper, and screen-savers.

PHYSICAL ACTIVITY AND EXERCISE

When my dad died in the fall of 1995, my sister-in-law Barbara insisted that we take a walk. Reluctantly, I went. Much to my surprise, walking was energizing. Being in the fresh air, moving around, and talking with an understanding companion were uplifting. Barbara told me that in Judaism, walking with a bereaved person is considered a *mitzvah*, a blessing. She and I walked and talked for hours, sometimes two or three times a day.

When Dick died in January, I could not walk outdoors, so I tried to spend a few minutes each day on the treadmill. Gradually I increased the time and then added my workouts. A few months later I was back to my full regimen.

Nearly all of my friends are walkers, and many go to the gym. We all agreed that exercise helped in many ways. When we didn't walk or work out, our days were not as good. We needed all those little endorphins jumping around, fending off the down times. Sometimes we had to push ourselves, but we always felt better knowing that we had done something good for ourselves. Exercise gave us energy. In retrospect it makes perfect sense that an early step toward normalcy was physical. We could hardly deal with the emotional.

One of us became a serious athlete. In the fall of 2000, after running in half a dozen races over the past two years and training for six months, Sara completed the 26-mile Chicago Marathon. She came in 20th out of the forty women competing in her age group. No runner has ever been more proud, and rightfully so.

WORK

For women who worked outside the home, their jobs provided a safe haven, social contacts, distraction, structure, and challenge. Sara and Sue continued in their careers and were fortified by this one element in their lives that remained constant when their worlds collapsed.

Some of us developed new talents and abilities in the workplace, either from necessity, choice, or both. Kay told me how she entered the business world. In 1956, Doug Johnson started a company that manufactured and sold a high tech product. Through hard work, the business prospered. Over the years Kay helped out from time to time. A few months after Doug's death, in 1983, Kay volunteered to work in the office. "I'm here to help out until you get organized," she told the staff. Kay laughed, "I never left . . . I'm still waiting!"

Kay stepped in, learned the business, and eventually ran the operation. "Right from the beginning, after Doug's death, work was my salvation." Eventually she brought in each of her three children and two of their spouses, one at a time. Through hard work, determination, and creative thinking, together they have built an extremely successful business. Each child has his or her own area of specialization and leadership. Kay is the financial manager.

I asked if the business has prospered. Proudly Kay described the company's growth. "Sales have increased tenfold since Doug's death. Back in 1983, we rented a small 4,000 square foot facility. Today we have an 18,000 square foot building."

Kay's tone changed as she continued, "Sometimes people ask how I can work day in and day out with my kids. I decided long ago that I must separate our personal and professional relationships. I can't be the Mother at work. We are colleagues and the company runs like a well-oiled machine." She chuckled, "Of course, every now and then I slip. A week ago I met with my oldest son, our CEO, for nearly two hours, discussing business. Just as I was leaving, I turned to him and said, 'You need to get a haircut!'"

The CEO of the company grinned and said, "Mom, get out!"

When the company moved into the present building, the previous owner, a car dealer, left a huge marquee outside. The day before the move, Kay drove up and read the new sign, *"Thanks to Dad for the start and to Mom for moving us forward."*

We both smiled. "You must be mighty proud of what you have done," I said.

"Of all the things I have accomplished, I think I am proudest of this because I had no preparation; I knew nothing about business. Now I love the work and the satisfaction it brings me."

SMALL VICTORIES

In our individual journeys, small victories became very important. On a visit with Sara, she told me a wonderful story.

"Last weekend I went to a wedding in Ohio. Even after seven years I still find going to weddings alone very difficult, but I was determined to plan every step, to protect myself from any stress, particularly in arranging the logistics. I even bought myself a new dress, to insure that I would feel good about me that evening.

"I flew to Cleveland, rented a car service to drive me to the small town where the wedding would be, and checked into the motel. Finally, at 60, I felt grown up! I enjoyed being by myself. I never thought I'd say that. The wedding was lovely. I didn't know a soul there so I was forced to talk to people, to reach out to total strangers. And I had a great time!

"I am seventy times better than I was seven years ago. No way could I have done that then or even five years ago. It was a learning experience for me. I overcame a fear, traveling and going to a wedding alone. I looked good, I had fun, I laughed. When my return transportation arrangements came unraveled, I didn't. I was resourceful and shifted to Plan B. I am really, really proud of myself. My attitude has changed. It's been a long haul, but after this weekend, I think I can handle just about anything."

Was this Sara talking? She certainly wasn't the Sara of only six months ago. She was proud of her accomplishment, and I was proud for her. Her tone of voice was strong, her words positive. That weekend had empowered her. Perhaps we all have a defining moment as Sara did. For her it was a seven-year journey, and she had made it.

Healing and becoming independent took time and hard work. From Sara I learned that when we have successes, we need to allow ourselves to acknowledge and honor our achievements. And we need to tell our friends because our victories can give them courage to stretch and to meet their own challenges.

PASSION

Joseph Campbell, a famous historian and writer, advised that in order to be happy, "follow your bliss, your passion." Some women found their passions by returning to earlier interests. A friend of mine named Anna lost her husband six years ago. When her husband died, she was devastated. During the early months of her loss, Anna and I walked and talked many times. One day she told me that she was signing up for ballroom dancing lessons. Dancing?

Anna explained that she had always loved to dance and she thought lessons might be fun—and they were. Soon, between lessons and practicing, she was spending many hours a week at the dance studio. Several months later, Anna announced that she was invited to participate in a dance competition in Las Vegas. With some apprehension she decided to go. Dressed in a stunning long, red dance costume and wearing dramatic makeup and hairdo, she won first-place awards for her tango, waltz, and fox trot. What a victory!

Hannah continues to be active in her church and is a mentor to a group of young mothers. She derives great joy from this service. She has also taken up watercolors again, plays golf several times a week in the summer, and goes cross-country skiing in the winter.

Ramona is exhilarated in her new career, teaching Spanish in several international corporations to executives who will need to use Spanish in their work. With her endless energy and diverse interests, Ramona has opened a small art gallery handling Wisconsin artists.

Shari established a college scholarship for worthy students as a memorial to Rex. This living tribute to her husband has given her great pride. Each time a student receives an award, she feels deep gratification.

And I have returned to my oldest and dearest passion, writing. I belong to a small group of writers who meet weekly at a local bookstore. From listening to the members' ideas and insights in critiquing each other's writing, I have learned a great deal.

Writing has brought me satisfaction and joy. Telling each woman's story has been a challenging and effective therapy. The greatest crisis of my life, my husband's death, became the force behind my greatest creativity. I cannot begin to wrestle with the irony.

MEMORIES

One afternoon about a year after Dick died, I thought about going through some old pictures. Remembering how this had stirred me up earlier, I had avoided the album shelf for many months. I felt stronger now. I really wanted to look at pictures.

The first was our wedding album. We both looked so happy. My tears poured out. I turned more pages, opened more albums and cried. As abruptly as they had come, my sobs subsided into quiet weeping, and I realized that my tears were no longer the tortuous tears of grief. These were tears of nostalgia for the life we had shared. As I looked through pictures of the two of us on a glacier in the Canadian Rockies, on safari in Africa, on a whitewater raft on the Colorado, I found myself smiling.

In that instant, I realized that my memories were making me happy. In those moments etched on film, I could see that Dick had been a happy man. I knew that his life had been filled with love, joy, and adventure. Perhaps this was the insight I needed that night. After months of mourning, seeing my husband's smiling face in our photos brought me great comfort.

For so long, the pictures in my consciousness were of the terrible day in Hawaii, my trip home, the funeral. Turning the pages of the albums, I knew that I was ready to bundle up the sad imprints and stow them in a small crevice of my memory. I was ready to welcome the happy images of times past.

L'DOR V'DOR

In the beginning, many people said to me, "Life goes on." Not for me, I thought. My life will be empty. But life did go on, and to my amazement, it was anything but empty.

In the summer of 1999, my daughter Margie bought a little house for herself, and she was the happiest I had ever seen her, despite her losses. She leaped into decorating projects and enjoyed every moment of home ownership. Her creativity and domesticity blossomed. She was proud of herself and I was delighted for her.

In the fall I visited Bruce and Jodi, my son and daughter-in-law, in New York. I was so excited to see them in their first home, a beautiful old farmhouse with updated additions, set in a wooded lot with a brook running through it. After the house tour, we stood in the kitchen. Bruce turned to me and grinned, "We have a birthday gift for you." I blinked. My birthday was months away. I glanced over at the table. No wrapped packages. My heart skipped a beat as I looked over at Jodi, who was smiling her warm, wonderful smile.

She said simply, "You're going to be a grandmother."

I burst into tears and hugged them both. Was this really happening to them, to me, to my family? I was speechless for a moment, then babbled my absolute joy. My first grandchild was due three days after my birthday, in May of 2000.

In Judaism we speak of *l'dor v'dor*, from generation to generation. For all the people we have lost, we would now have a new member of our family, a continuation of line and life.

As I lay in bed that night, ecstatic at the news, I had a sudden backwash of emotion. "Why can't Dick be here to give Bruce an 'Attaboy!' and beam with pride? Why can't Jake be here to see his first grandchild?" Then another question came into my mind, "Why am I allowed to have this joy?" My only answer to all these questions was, "*B'shert.*"

Since the minute Jessica was born, three weeks after my birthday, I have experienced a joy I could never have imagined. This adorable, bright, energetic little girl is a miracle, a blessing that has come into all our lives. And if this grandmother brags and coos and carries on overly much, I forgive myself because I love her not only for myself, but also for the grandfathers she will never know.

ACCEPTANCE

Surviving the death of a spouse, and becoming whole, is a long process, an odyssey of many twists, turns, plateaus, leaps, steps forward, steps backward. All nine of us have traversed the phases of shock, anger, denial, and eventually acceptance, growth, and renewal. Finally, step by step, we are evolving and emerging anew.

Desolation is now insight. Despair and emptiness are hope and creativity. Self-pity is now resilience and self-realization. Fear is strength and courage.

We have been transformed. We are more independent, decisive, self-confident, and courageous. We have a clearer vision of who we are and of our capabilities. When we look back and see how far we have come, we are astounded, proud, and grateful.

We know that the best way we can honor our husbands is to carry on as they would want us to. They would want us to live happy and fulfilling lives. Perhaps Kay said it best, "It's what Doug would have expected of me . . . I don't want to fail him or me."

Each in our own way, we have created a whole cloth, each different. For all of us, the threads will hold; the fabric is strong.

"CHOOSE LIFE"

At the Shabbat service on the evening of Dick's funeral, Rabbi Silberg read a passage praising God for the gift of Life. Then he read from Deuteronomy 30:10, "I have put before you life and death, blessing and curse. Choose life. . . ."

Through my tears, I looked up and blinked. Did I only imagine that the rabbi was looking directly and intently at me, with a slight smile? On the saddest day of my life, the day we buried my husband, I was hearing that life is our most precious gift. The rabbi was telling me that I will need, and will have, the strength to go on with my life and it will be a good one.

How often I recall those two simple words, "Choose life." This is the affirmation that all who grieve must embrace.

We have raised the cup of wine and said, "*L'chaim*—TO LIFE!"

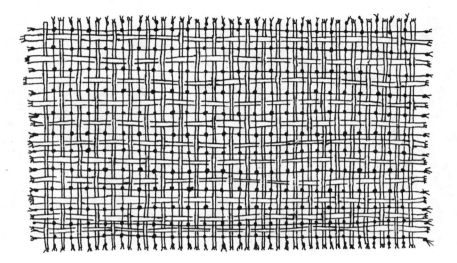

References

1. Dr. Reinhold Niebuhr, *The Serenity Prayer,* Union Theological Seminary, New York City, 1932.
2. Brian L. Weiss, M.D., *Many Lives, Many Masters*, Simon & Schuster, New York, 1988.
3. James Van Praagh, *Talking to Heaven,* Signet Penguin Putnam, New York, 1997.
4. Robert Burns, "To a Mouse," *Bartlett's Quotations,* Little, Brown and Co., p. 390, 1955.
5. Brothers, Dr. Joyce, *Widowed,* Ballantine Books, New York, 1990.
6. Richard Carlson, *Don't Sweat the Small Stuff . . . and it's all small stuff,* Hyperion, New York, 1997.
7. Martha Whitmore Hickman, *Healing After Loss—Daily Meditations for Working through Grief,* Avon Books Inc., New York, 1994.
8. Rabbi Joseph Telushkin, *Jewish Literacy,* William Morrow & Co., New York, 1991.
9. Native American Poem, from *God Makes the Rivers to Flow, Selections from the Sacred Literature of the World,* Eknath Easwaran (ed.), The Blue Mountain Center of Meditation, Nilgiri Press, Tomales, California, 1991.
10. Earl A. Grollman, *Living When a Loved One Has Died,* Beacon Press, Boston, 1995.
11. Naomi Levy, *To Begin Again: The Journey Toward Comfort, Strength, and Faith in Difficult Times,* Alfred A. Knopf, New York, 1998.
12. Barry Unsworth, *Sacred Hunger,* W. W. Norton and Co., New York, 1993.

Index